A Culture of Caring

A Culture of Caring

A Suicide Prevention Guide for Schools (K–12)

Theodora Schiro

ROWMAN & LITTLEFIELD
Lanham • Boulder • New York • London

Published by Rowman & Littlefield
An imprint of The Rowman & Littlefield Publishing Group, Inc.
4501 Forbes Boulevard, Suite 200, Lanham, Maryland 20706
www.rowman.com

6 Tinworth Street, London SE11 5AL

British Library Cataloguing in Publication Information Available

Library of Congress Cataloging-in-Publication Data

Library of Congress Control Number: 2019956612
ISBN 978-1-4758-4448-1 (cloth)
ISBN 978-1-4758-4450-4 (electronic)

Contents

Foreword

In 2011, I was a fellow colleague and principal with Theo Schiro when she and Steve experienced the loss of their son. It was a sad and tragic time for them, and along with their loved ones we mourned with them. Since that time, it has been inspirational to witness the resilience of both Theo and Steve as they advocate and educate others on the warning signs of suicide to help prevent it from occurring in other families.

As an educational leader, I know that candid, straightforward, and succinct work like this is needed for educational leaders, parents, stakeholders, teachers, counselors, social workers, faith-based leaders, and others to help break the stigma of suicide and depression and to better support, dialogue with, and care for others in the prevention of suicide.

This book is a vulnerable and heartfelt plea from not only an educator and leader, but also a mother. The resources, tools, and information in this book can help schools and districts rally around and create plans to better support all students and help families and communities talk about mental illness and depression in their efforts to prevent suicide.

—Cort Monroe, EdD
Assistant Superintendent of Support Services
Queen Creek Unified School District

Preface

THE STORY OF JOSS

Not long ago, my life was fairly normal. I had a loving husband and two smart kids. After twenty years as a classroom teacher, I had finally reached my goal of being a principal for an elementary school. I learned how to be an effective school leader and thrived in my belief that I was making a difference in the lives of the children I was responsible for. I looked forward to going to work each morning, knowing that planning and preparing for the unexpected was impossible, but preparing just the same.

Shattered

I never saw this one coming. On March 28, 2011, my life was shattered. Painfully, irrevocably shattered. It would never be normal again.

As I was getting ready to leave school and head home at the end of the day, my husband called. He told me to come home right away. I asked what was wrong, but he wouldn't say. All he said was, "Just come now. Hurry."

With my stomach churning, I drove home as fast as I could, wondering what could have happened. I was totally unprepared for the reality of what I found when I got there. Fire trucks, police cars, and other emergency vehicles were scattered in the street around our house. As I got to the front door, my husband stopped me and said the police wouldn't let us go inside. Then he told me why.

He had heard a gunshot inside the house just as he was getting home from work. Shocked, he searched the house until he found the body of our twenty-one-year-old son. He had taken his own life moments before.

A senior at the local state university, Joss would have graduated in just a few months with degrees in both psychology and biology. He was a passionate and brilliant student, fascinated by brain research, and had plans to continue his studies of neuroscience. Looking back, I believe he thought he would find clues to his own mental illness through his studies of the brain.

Picking Up the Pieces

The aftermath of that day was horrible. Both Steve and I struggled with unexpected tears and bouts of intense grief for many months. We blamed ourselves for not being better parents and searched for reasons why we had not seen the signs that led to our son's final choice. After reading what seemed like hundreds of books and articles about suicide, we finally began to understand that Joss's death was the result of mental illness. The signs were there—we just didn't recognize them. Although we couldn't go back in time and change what happened, we wanted to help other families avoid becoming survivors of suicide loss.

There is a ripple effect for every suicide. Not only is the immediate family affected, but friends, relatives, teachers, coworkers, and everyone who knows about it is touched by the loss. As I learned more about the causes and ways to prevent suicide, I vowed to do everything possible to raise awareness, attack the stigma, and teach others the things I wish I had known before I lost my only son.

The Signs We Didn't See

Since that awful day, my husband and I have become educated in suicide risk factors and learned to recognize the warning signs. Looking back, Joss started showing signs of mental illness as early as ten years old. He had anxiety, which we saw as difficulty making decisions. We were patient with him, but never even thought of getting a medical evaluation.

He told me one day that he wanted to kill himself. He was in fifth grade then. I told the counselor at the school about that. He worked part-time at other schools in the district and was very busy. He gave me a little pink laminated card he thought might be helpful but never found time to talk to my son. The card had information about emergencies and some phone numbers, but I don't really remember much about it. Joss didn't mention suicide again, and over time I didn't give it much thought.

Joss hated change. Transitions from elementary to middle school and then to high school were awfully hard for him. We saw it as insecurity. Looking back, I'm pretty sure he suffered from anxiety and could have benefited from medication and therapy. Middle school was torture for him—he hated going to school every day. We didn't really know why but made him go. The guidance counselor at the school was a friend, and we figured she would look out for him if he needed help.

Joss didn't like high school either. He went every day, got good grades, and earned a scholarship to the local state university. But during the second half of his senior year, with a huge transition to college looming, he started a steep decline. Joss just didn't want to get out of bed. He stopped caring about his grades and missed so many days that he was at risk of not graduating. His behavior changed dramatically, and he was often belligerent and angry. I contacted his teachers but got little response. The two that got back to me said he was talking back in class and not doing homework.

Then he attempted to take his life. One Saturday when he was home alone, Joss took a bunch of pills. Fortunately, when we got home that afternoon, he told my husband what he had done and we were able to get him to the emergency room in time.

After that, Joss agreed to go to counseling and started taking antidepressants. He never found a counselor he liked and gave up trying. He would not go to a psychiatrist but went to the family doctor instead. Our general practitioner prescribed medication, monitored it for a few months, and then continued to refill the prescription on request without ever seeing Joss again.

Joss made the transition to the local university and even seemed to enjoy his classes. He preferred to live at home rather than in a dorm—again a big sign of anxiety. By his senior year, he had made some close friends and seemed destined for success. But another big transition was coming soon—graduation and leaving college to find a job.

During spring break, while he seemed happy and in a good mood, Joss planned his exit carefully. He spent more time with the family, saying goodbye in his own way without anyone knowing that he was leaving soon. He went to parties and gave away some of his prized possessions to special friends. He bought a handgun and hid it in his closet. You know what happened next.

If Only We Had Known

If only we had known then what we know now. Looking back, the signs were glaring. We might have started counseling and treatment after the first signs emerged when Joss was ten. Just like any other disease, the prognosis is much better if you catch it early. But we can't go back in time and change anything.

So instead, Steve and I are working hard to teach educators how to recognize the warning signs and take action. Because they spend so much time with children, people who work in schools can be proactive and take steps to prevent tragedies like ours from happening to other families. If they have the knowledge to recognize signs and risk factors, the courage to speak up, and the resources to find help when they see a child struggling with depression and anxiety or other mental illness, educators can be lifesavers.

Steve, a former classroom teacher, works closely with our local suicide prevention agency. He teaches about suicide prevention by giving presentations to students, teachers, and parents at high schools and community centers. He serves as a panel facilitator and gives presentations on suicide prevention at numerous conferences. He also helps survivors of suicide loss find the resources they need to begin their journeys of recovery.

My opportunity to teach others about suicide prevention came when, after leaving my career as an educator, I decided to become a professional writer. By tapping into Steve's knowledge and experience, interviewing experts we have met during our search for answers, and doing plenty of research, I have gathered information that will help schools and districts prevent suicide.

This book was created as a resource for educators who want to know how to get started and what steps to take to create a suicide prevention plan that will work for their schools and districts. It is written from my perspective as a school principal and survivor of suicide loss, not an expert in psychology, counseling, or suicide prevention. I hope that any teacher, school counselor, principal, or district administrator can pick up this book, flip to a chapter, and easily find helpful answers to the questions they are likely to have about what schools can do to prevent suicide.

Introduction

When my son died by suicide in 2011, my husband and I were totally shocked and unprepared. In the following months and years, we vowed to learn as much as we could about suicide prevention and spread the word to raise awareness, hoping that we could prevent other parents from suffering the way we have.

You will notice frequent references to the American Foundation for Suicide Prevention (AFSP) and commentary from several AFSP experts throughout this book. While there are other excellent organizations dedicated to suicide prevention, AFSP was the first one we turned to for answers. We became involved in advocacy through the opportunities the organization offers to survivors. Because their emphasis is on research, education, advocacy, and supporting survivors of suicide loss, they are a comprehensive source of information for those interested in learning about suicide prevention.

In researching the topic of suicide prevention for this book, I found there is even more information and support available than I imagined. I am excited to share what I've learned with everyone who works in schools.

It is my sincere hope that by informing and educating others, we can do for suicide prevention what other activists have done for breast cancer research. Think of the word "breast." Do you remember when it was inappropriate to mention a woman's breast in polite conversation? Now the word is memorialized by pink ribbons and printed everywhere from yogurt containers to car commercials. If we can stop the stigma, suicide prevention could become as common as breast cancer awareness. It will be integrated into wellness conversations and something that people naturally accept.

This book is designed as a handbook for busy educators. Having spent more than thirty-six years as a teacher, principal, and administrator, I know how limited time is for anyone who works in schools. Each chapter stands alone and does not have to be read in sequence. Some information is repeated in different chapters for that reason. Resources and descriptions of programs relevant to each chapter are organized by topic. Most of these resources can be easily accessed online by simple searches or using the URLs as listed.

Whether you use the information in this book to create your own plan or just glance through it to get ideas, any school community that takes suicide prevention seriously can readily access the knowledge, tools, and resources to save lives.

Chapter One

A Brief History of Suicide Prevention

Throughout our history, the act of suicide has carried a stigma. The person who commits suicide is thought to be selfish and weak, with no regard for those left behind. Whether the method used was a firearm, hanging, overdose, asphyxiation, or some other lethal means, the death is considered an act of cowardice—the easy way out.

Because of society's negative perception of suicide, family members fear ostracism, and the death is shrouded in silence. Many survivors of suicide loss suffer through their grief alone, ashamed to seek help or talk about their pain and guilt. Believing it's best just to move on, the name of the person who died by suicide is simply not brought up, leaving the memories and relationships with the loved one to private reflection.

People who struggle with suicidal thoughts are reluctant to seek help, feeling that they will be seen as weak or somehow flawed. Fearing disclosure of depression or other mental illness may cost them their careers, many refuse to get treatment and struggle with their disease in the vain hope that it will pass. Often choosing self-medication in the form of drugs or alcohol, they battle their demons alone.

Obviously, ignoring suicide doesn't make it go away. It is a leading cause of death across all age groups. Suicides outnumber homicides by three to two. The link to mental illness has been backed by irrefutable scientific evidence for years, but the concept of preventing suicide was not on the public radar until fairly recently.

EMERGENCE OF SUICIDE PREVENTION

A discovery of hundreds of suicide notes in the Los Angeles coroner's office by two doctors in 1949 led to years of investigation and study. Funded by grants from the U.S. Public Health Service, a team of dedicated doctors in Los Angeles opened the first Suicide Prevention Center (SPC) in the United States in 1958.[1]

The work done by the SPC laid the foundation for understanding and preventing suicide in the United States. As the concept of researching and preventing suicide emerged, it was addressed as a community problem. The perception was that suicide prevention should be treated as first aid in the time of crisis, and close family members or partners should be involved.

Several primary areas of focus evolved. Teams of doctors continued to research and study the signs and symptoms of suicide risk, with an emphasis on psychological autopsies. The SPC provided a 24-hour call line staffed by trained clinical associates to help people who were in crisis. Psychiatrists, psychologists, nurses, and social workers addressed the needs of suicidal patients and their families. The SPC offered consultation services and training to other health agencies, believing their model could be used to help others across the country. Perhaps most important, the SPC attempted to change the social attitudes about suicide.

The National Institute of Mental Health (NIMH) established the Center for Studies of Suicide Prevention in 1966 and assembled a task force to study the issues. The results, presented in a 1973 report, *Suicide Prevention in the '70s,*[2] emphasized the need to create a common language and standardized reporting procedures. By then some two hundred suicide prevention centers had opened around the country, but most lacked consistent research-based training in suicidology.

Nonprofit organizations joined the cause, complementing the expansion of prevention centers. Dr. Edwin Shneidman, one of the founders of the Los Angeles SPC, established the American Association of Suicidology (AAS) in 1968. Devoted to research, education, and practice in suicidology, AAS became the clearinghouse for research and information. The organization developed standards for certification of crisis centers. In 1987, a group of survivors of suicide loss and scientists formed a national nonprofit organization, the American Foundation for Suicide Prevention. AFSP was dedicated to understanding and preventing suicide through research, education, and advocacy. Driven by their own losses, another group of survivors formed SAVE, Suicide Awareness Voices of Education, in 1989. Their goal was to increase public awareness and education, reduce stigma, and provide resources for other survivors of suicide loss.

A sharp increase in suicides among young people between the ages of fifteen and twenty-four caught the nation's attention and led to further research and increased involvement by the U.S. Department of Health and Human Services. Public outcry resulted in the creation of a Task Force on Youth Suicide in 1989.[3]

A list of suicidal risk factors was identified, but at the same time researchers recognized that youth responded differently to treatment models used for adults. Concluding that existing data on causes and prevention strategies barely scratched the surface, the recommendations emphasized that more research was needed on multiple aspects of youth suicide.

Along with accurate reporting of completed suicide and suicide attempts, the task force studied identification of youth risk factors, including mental illness, drug and alcohol abuse, and primary prevention and treatment specifically for young people. They recommended that crisis services should be staffed by personnel trained in working with teens and young adults and in understanding the unique needs of minorities and LGBTQ youth. Further recommendations included education of the public, teachers, parents, and media, effective school-based prevention programs, and emergency treatment for suicide attempts.

Working with the World Health Organization (WHO), the United Nations (UN) called attention to suicide as an international concern. Offering guidelines for member nations to develop national prevention strategies, the UN published *Prevention of Suicide: Guidelines for the Formulation and Implementation of National Strategies* in 1996.[4]

Spurred by grassroots efforts and collaboration among government agencies and the Suicide Prevention Advocacy Network (SPAN), community leaders joined researchers, physicians and other health experts, survivors of suicide loss, and policymakers at a national conference on suicide prevention in Reno, Nevada, in 1998. The following year, the surgeon general issued the *Call to Action to Prevent Suicide*.[5] Based on the findings from the Reno conference, a new framework was introduced: Awareness, Intervention, and Methodology (AIM). Recognizing that improving mental health had to be a priority, Surgeon General David Snatcher called on each community to use the AIM blueprint to develop their own programs.

Recommendations were segmented into three parts, with specific examples of suggested actions. Awareness: increase the public's awareness of the risk factors of suicide and emphasize that suicide is a public health problem that can be prevented. Intervention: improve services and programs, starting with training primary care providers and including all human service professionals, community helpers, and families of people showing signs of suicide risk. Methodology: advance the science of suicide prevention.

With growing recognition of suicide as a serious public health problem, communities were urged to take action. Developed using the AIM model and released in 2001, the *National Strategy for Suicide Prevention*[6] provided a common point of reference, a resource for advocacy, and awareness of the needs of those affected by suicide.

A 2002 report, *Reducing Suicide: A National Imperative*,[7] issued four primary recommendations: create a national network of suicide research labs to expand research across larger and more diverse populations, promote national monitoring and reporting of completed suicide and attempted suicides, improve training and tools for primary health care providers, and develop and implement effective suicide prevention programs.

Increasing awareness and interest in suicide prevention accelerated the pace of research not only on suicide prevention but on the mental health delivery system in the United States. Recognizing the limitations in the flawed mental health care system that allows mental illness to go untreated because of the stigma of mental illness, treatment limits and expense, and a fragmented mental health delivery system, the New Freedom Commission on Mental Health proposed specific goals in its 2003 *Achieving the Promise: Transforming Mental Health Care in America*.[8]

Charting the Future of Suicide Prevention came out in 2010[9] and offered a positive view of progress at the community level toward the goals of the National Strategy for Suicide Prevention (NSSP) issued in 2001 by the surgeon general. Public awareness increased along with the willingness to discuss suicide more openly.

The establishment of the Suicide Prevention Resource Center and the Suicide Prevention Lifeline along with advocacy and training for members of the public expanded access to suicide prevention. However, despite the combined efforts of government, health care workers, researchers, schools, and community leaders, suicide rates did not change. Recommendations for continued research, training, mental health care, and leadership offered hope for the future.

ACTIVE PREVENTION EFFORTS

Established in 2002, the Suicide Prevention Resource Center (SPRC) serves as a national resource center dedicated to supporting the National Strategy for Suicide Prevention. Funded by the U.S. Department of Health and Human Services' Substance Abuse and Mental Health Services Administration (SAMHSA) and located at the Education Development Center, SPRC offers a broad range of services and support.[10] Among the available resources are webinars on how to create suicide prevention programs and how to apply for Garrett Lee Smith (GLS) grants for suicide prevention funding.

As a result of the 2001 National Strategy for Suicide Prevention, most states developed suicide prevention plans based on public-private partnerships. State and local government agencies work with private sector groups to plan, develop, implement, and evaluate programs in communities. Plans are evaluated and updated annually.

The Garrett Lee Smith Memorial Act (2004) was perhaps the most significant legislation passed for intervention and prevention of youth suicide. Currently funded and administered by SAMHSA, suicide prevention grants are awarded every year to states, tribes, territories, colleges, and universities. Grants have supported hundreds of youth suicide prevention programs, tribal initiatives, and college programs since its inception. [11]

The Joshua Omvig Veterans Suicide Prevention Act followed in 2007, focusing on efforts to prevent suicide among veterans. Mandating training on suicide risk factors and crisis response for VA health care workers, the bill required 24-hour mental health care for veterans, outreach counselors to coordinate with local emergency and mental health organizations, and a peer counseling program.

The National Suicide Prevention Lifeline, 1-800-273-TALK (8255), started taking calls in 2005. Connecting people to local crisis centers across the country, the Lifeline offers more than crisis intervention services. The organization provides best practices for professionals and resources for individuals and communities. Active social media campaigns are designed to raise awareness for individuals, communities, physicians, emergency workers, military, and more. Groups can work with the Lifeline to create custom messages tailored to their own needs. [12]

Using the National Violent Death Reporting System (NVDRS), called for in the 2001 National Strategy, the Center for Disease Control (CDC) collects information on violent deaths by state. Expanding from six states in 2002 to forty in 2015, the NVDRS provides usable data to state agencies. While numbers fluctuate from year to year, in 2015 more than 44,000 people died by suicide in the United States, and homicide took more than 17,000 lives.

Data from death certificates, police reports, medical examiner and coroner reports, and crime labs are pooled together into an anonymous database available to the public. Referred to as violence surveillance data, information on "who, when, where, and how" is collected with the intention of finding out why the violent deaths occurred. Gathering facts about circumstances surrounding a suicide death, including mental illness, stress factors, relationships, or financial problems, may help us understand the underlying causes. Comprehensive reports are issued each year, allowing practitioners in suicide prevention to use current data to inform prevention programs, policies, and practices.

THE ACTION ALLIANCE

Formed in 2010 to advance the National Strategy, the National Action Alliance for Suicide Prevention (Action Alliance)[13] is supported by the SPRC and involved with over 250 organizations. With the goal of reducing the annual suicide rate 20 percent by 2025, the Action Alliance has made progress in several areas.

Working with the media has started to change the public conversation. Messaging about suicide has shifted from sensational drama to promoting social support, connectedness, treatment, hope, resilience, and recovery. The phrase "died by suicide" is slowly replacing the accusatory "committed suicide" when reporting a suicide death. Other accomplishments include improving suicide surveillance data, advancing suicide prevention among working-aged adults, and the creation of a toolkit to show health care workers how to follow the Zero Suicide approach.

Ten years after the National Strategy was released in 2001, the Action Alliance assembled a task force to study the results of the original plan and recommend a course of action for the next decade. Published in 2012, the updated National Strategy[14] provides a guide for suicide prevention founded on current research and changing the perspective on suicide prevention. The comprehensive approach includes a shift from thinking of suicide as a mental health issue to a health issue that should be addressed at many levels.

PROGRESS AND PROBLEMS

In December 2017, SAMHSA published a report on the Action Alliance's assessment of the progress made on the National Strategy for Suicide Prevention. The results were shocking. Suicide rates increased 28 percent from 2000 to 2015, despite collective efforts toward preventing suicide in the United States. The only conclusion to draw is that the implementation of a comprehensive approach has not been adequate. The report recommends further actions to increase the effective implementation of the National Strategy.

On closer inspection of the data over time and comparison to prevention activity as reported in the 2010 *Charting the Future of Suicide Prevention: A Progress Review of the National Strategy and Recommendations for the Decade Ahead*, significant progress in developing programs and best practices is evident. The problem is that although the information is easily accessible, few organizations have built standard policies or protocols around suicide prevention.

Several actionable recommendations emerged from the most recent research findings. The National Strategy was created as a broad guide for community-based prevention, but future models could be more effective if a clear blueprint with step-by-step implementation procedures were available, similar to the toolkit already in use for health care systems in the SPRC's Zero Suicide program.

Once the states, tribes, and communities know what to do, somebody has to be in charge of making it happen. A sustainable infrastructure with strong, active leadership at state, tribal, and community levels is critical to the success of an effective suicide prevention program. It would also be valuable to share strategies and collaborate with other organizations rather than working in isolation.

Some of the organizations that built their infrastructures have seen measurable results and a reduction in suicide rates in targeted populations. Their work serves as an example of effective implementation. But lacking sustainable funding other than grants or donations, and without community buy-in or sustainable leadership, the best efforts of suicide prevention practitioners often flounder.

Moving forward, monitoring and collecting data to evaluate the effectiveness of local, state, and tribal programs on a regular basis would help identify areas in need of improvement. Comparing progress made in suicide prevention to that associated with the K–12 education world, educators know that teachers depend on frequent formative assessments to determine student progress and guide instruction. Waiting until the end for the summative evaluation results helps us see where they've been, but not where they need to go.

FACTS AND FIGURES

Suicide can be prevented. Awareness is the first step. Most people are shocked when they see statistics on suicide deaths for the first time.[15]

- Someone in the United States dies by suicide every 11.89 minutes.
- There are 129 suicides in the United States daily.
- Americans attempt suicide an estimated 1.3 million times annually.
- Of those who die by suicide, 90 percent had a diagnosable psychiatric disorder at the time of their death.
- In 2016, firearms were the most common method of death by suicide, accounting for more than half (51 percent) of all suicide deaths.
- Since 2009, the number of deaths by suicide surpasses the number of deaths caused by vehicle accidents each year.
- Nearly 16 percent of students in grades nine to twelve report considering suicide, and half report those thoughts have led to at least one suicide attempt in the past year.

- For every woman who dies by suicide, more than three men die by suicide. Women are three times more likely to attempt suicide.
- More than 47,000 Americans die by suicide every year. Suicide is the tenth leading cause of death in the United States
    - ♦ the second leading cause of death for ages 1 to 44
    - ♦ the fifth leading cause of death for ages 45 to 59
    - ♦ the rate among America Indian/Alaska Native adolescents and young adults ages 15 to 24 is 1.5 times the national average
- Veterans comprise 18 percent of suicides.
- Suicide and self-injury cost Americans an estimated $69 billion in medical bills and lost productivity annually.
- A single suicide costs an estimated $1 million in medical costs and lost productivity.

Suicide is a leading cause of death in the United States. It is a preventable public health problem. By continuing to invest in suicide prevention, education, and research and working with state, tribal, and community efforts, we can save the lives of thousands of Americans each year and prevent the loss, pain, and suffering of those who love them.

Chapter Two

The Current State of Suicide Prevention in Schools

My life felt so cluttered and obstructed that I could hardly breathe. I inhabited a closed, concentrated world, airless and without exits. I had entered the closed world of suicide, and my life was being lived for me by forces I couldn't control.

—Alfred Alvarez, *The Savage God: A Study of Suicide*

When a child dies by suicide, parents blame themselves. No matter what their background, level of education, or profession, most are totally unprepared. They may have seen the signs but did not recognize them. If they had known what to look for, they could have. The clues were there for years.

Although the act itself may seem to be an impulsive reaction to temporary emotional distress, suicide is rarely spontaneous. It's the result of multiple factors converging at the same time. Usually involving depression or other mental illness, a suicide death is triggered by pain impossible to bear.

We can't undo the suffering of those who have lost a loved one. But by educating ourselves about warning signs and risk factors and knowing how to find help when a person is struggling, we can save lives by learning how to prevent suicide.

WE CAN PREVENT SUICIDE

Suicide is the second leading cause of death for young people ages ten to twenty-four.[1] Results from the 2015 Youth Risk Behavior Survey show that more than one in six high school students has considered attempting suicide, and 8 percent of them did attempt suicide.[2]

Stop and think about that for a moment. If you are in a classroom with a group of thirty students, five of them have thought about taking their own lives, and two or three of them have attempted to. You know those kids; they have names and faces—they are not just statistics. If you could identify who was struggling, would you reach out to help them?

Ninety percent of young people who die by suicide have a mental health condition at the time of their death, often undiagnosed or untreated. Because children and teens spend so much of their time in school, trained teachers and other school personnel could identify students who may be at risk and get them the help they need.

A school culture that promotes emotional well-being and connectedness is an important protective factor. Educators who know how to identify students at risk for suicide make referrals to school counselors or psychologists and teach students to refer themselves or their friends. Proactive comprehensive policies and procedures guide their actions. If a tragedy happens, they're prepared to respond appropriately and provide support to the school and community.

EXPERT COMMENTARY: NICOLE GIBSON, DIRECTOR OF STATE POLICY AND GRASSROOTS ADVOCACY, AMERICAN FOUNDATION FOR SUICIDE PREVENTION (AFSP)

In her role as director of state policy and grassroots advocacy, Nicole Gibson oversees AFSP's state and local advocacy efforts. She works closely with AFSP chapters and volunteers across the country, helping them navigate the intricacies of advocacy in their states and communities.

With Nicole's support, dedicated volunteers have successfully advocated for legislation in their states. New laws for suicide prevention training and policies for schools are passed each year.

In collaboration with several other national groups, Nicole was instrumental in creating a comprehensive Model School District Policy for Suicide Prevention. Schools and districts use the model to develop effective prevention policies.

The Current State of Suicide Prevention in Schools

"In terms of advocacy we've seen amazing progress and rallying at the state level to increase school attention on the issue and build capacity within schools to be able to better handle suicide prevention, intervention, and post-intervention."

There is a growing awareness of the importance of making sure there's a support structure of adults within the school who have been informed and know what to do when they're presented with a young person who may be at risk for suicide. They need to be able to recognize what the risk factors and warning signs are, and subsequently know what to do when they see them.

When AFSP started working in state advocacy in 2011, only nine states had anything on the books about having school personnel trained in suicide prevention or how to recognize signs of students at risk and make referrals. Since then, that number has increased substantially. Now thirty-two states have laws about suicide prevention in schools. In recent years, eighteen states have also passed laws about having policies in place for prevention, intervention, and postvention. Momentum really has picked up—that's incredible growth in a short time.

AFSP has put out model legislation for suicide prevention in schools, and that is reflected as many states are incorporating suggested language. Not necessarily in its entirety, but pieces of that model are reflected in a large number of those state laws now. That also means that state legislators who are dedicated to getting the best information they can are relying on experts in the field and looking to AFSP as a resource.

There's good reason for optimism. AFSP has had incredible partnerships with associations that work in the education space, like the National Association of School Psychologists (NASP) and the American School Counselor Association (ASCA). Knowing that not all schools have mental health professionals, AFSP has been supporting policies at the state level to try and expand the mental health and behavioral health care workforce. For example, there are initiatives in progress that would create a loan forgiveness program to encourage people to go into the field and work in underserved areas.

The *Model School District Policy* that was developed in partnership with school counselors and school psychologists was written with the understanding that not all schools will have a school-based mental health professional on site. Schools that don't have a full-time school-based mental health professional are encouraged to develop MOUs[3] or something similar so they can connect students who are identified as at potential risk with services available in the community.

Shortage of Sustainable Funding

"One of the biggest barriers that we have to passing legislation that impacts suicide prevention in schools is that states are very reluctant to pass an unfunded mandate."

Lack of funding as it relates to state infrastructure that supports suicide prevention, in general, is a major barrier. Schools are told that they need to train their staff, they need to develop policy, and they need to educate students. But if the state's not able to give them money to do that, it's very difficult.

In statewide suicide prevention efforts, a lot of states rely on grants as the sole or primary funding source. At the federal level, most youth suicide prevention money comes as grants from the Garrett Lee Smith Memorial Suicide Prevention Program, funded by the Substance Abuse and Mental Health Services Administration (SAMHSA). SAMHSA also funds National Strategy for Suicide Prevention (NSSP) grants and Zero Suicide grants. [4] However, none of that money is guaranteed past the end of the grant.

Sometimes states establish really strong programs using these grant dollars. But if the state doesn't have a dedicated line item in the budget for suicide prevention or other diverse sources of funding, those programs risk being cut once the grant goes away. Sustainable and diverse funding for suicide prevention initiatives is a challenge across the board in this country.

Access to Mental Health Care

"Access to mental healthcare is a barrier. There are not enough health professionals in many schools and communities to work with young people and their families."

Suicide prevention efforts typically encourage parents and guardians to seek help from a mental health professional when they suspect their child may be at risk for suicide. Families need to have access to a professional locally, not someone who is hours away. They need to have insurance that covers mental health care the same way it covers other types of health care. AFSP has advocated for mental health parity for years. Access is a huge issue geographically and financially.

The other piece of that puzzle is to make sure that the mental health professional is equipped to handle suicide risk. There's no minimum standard across the country for mental health professionals to have suicide-specific training. Many assume training in how to recognize and treat depression, anxiety, and other mental health conditions is sufficient to prevent suicide, but research is showing that treating suicidal thoughts and behavior specifically is most effective. There is still a lot of work to do in that area.

Nine states right now have laws in place that say certain health care professionals must have mandatory training in suicide assessment, treatment, and management. There's a disconnect there if in thirty-two states educators have to be trained on suicide prevention, but a health professional has to be trained for it in only nine states. What happens when those educators refer their students to a health professional, and there is no guarantee that the professional has acquired suicide-specific training in their professional education or career development?

Capacity

We all have a role to play in suicide prevention, but how can we build capacity within the schools to take this on? Schools have to do so much, and there's hesitancy to take on one more thing, particularly when resources are scarce. Part of AFSP's role as the leading organization in this space is to make it as easy as possible for schools. That's what the Model Policy is about, along with all of the educational materials available to schools and the support of AFSP's nationwide network of chapters.

What Does the Most Effective State Statute for Suicide Prevention in Schools Look Like?

AFSP has created model legislation for states to use as a guide. If a state does not currently have adequate prevention laws in place, the model legislation template below is a useful tool. Updated versions will be available as the model is revised in future years.

AFSP Model Legislation: Suicide Prevention in Schools[5]

(1) Beginning in the 2018–2019 school year, the State Board/Department of Education shall adopt rules to require that all public school personnel receive at least 2 hours of suicide awareness and prevention training each year.* This training shall be provided within the framework of existing in-service training programs offered by the State Board/Department of Education or as part of required professional development activities.

(2) The State *Board/Department* of Education shall, in consultation with *state agency/coalition charged with coordinating state suicide prevention activities, other stakeholders, and suicide prevention experts*, develop a list of approved training materials to fulfill the requirements of this Section.

   a. Approved materials shall include training on how to identify appropriate mental health services both within the school and also within the larger community, and when and how to refer youth and their families to those services.
   b. Approved materials may include programs that can be completed through self-review of suitable suicide prevention materials.

(3)

   a. Each public school district shall adopt a policy on student suicide prevention. Such policies shall be developed in consultation with school and community stakeholders, school-employed mental health professionals, and suicide prevention experts, and shall, at a minimum, address procedures relating to suicide prevention, intervention, and postvention.

   b. To assist school districts in developing policies for student suicide prevention, the Department of Education shall develop and maintain a model policy to serve as a guide for school districts in accordance with this section.

(4)

   a. No person shall have a cause of action for any loss or damage caused by any act or omission resulting from the implementation of the provisions of this Section or resulting from any training, or lack thereof, required by this Section.

   b. The training, or lack thereof, required by the provisions of this Section shall not be construed to impose any specific duty of care.

*In those states where the legislature must amend section (1) to require training less often, for example, once every 5 years, or that remove a frequency requirement entirely, a new section will be added that states:

> The State *Board/Department* of Education shall adopt rules to require that all newly employed public school personnel receive at least 2 hours of suicide awareness and prevention training within 12 months of their date of hire.

Evaluating Suicide Prevention Efforts in Schools

> "That's the challenge that we have in suicide prevention all the time, to prove that what we're doing is effective. We basically have to prove that something didn't occur."

For now, the evidence of the effectiveness of state law changes is mostly anecdotal. It's hard to tie it to an actual reduction in suicide rates because of the lag in suicide data. If a law is passed, for example, in 2017 or 2018, we're still relying on suicide data from 2015 and 2016. To do that type of analysis you have to look at a few years back.

Also complicating the research is that young people are living within systems, and the school system is just one of those. It's hard to tie a change in the school system to an overall reduction in suicide for that age group because they're touched by so many other variables. In the future, researchers could design a study that would look at those variables in more detail.

Effective Prevention Models

In Utah and South Carolina, AFSP advocacy volunteers have set a good example of how to support the implementation of a state mandate for training and for policy. In both cases, the AFSP chapter has partnered with the state's department of education to offer training on a broad scale.

It's done online in the state of Utah. They incorporate AFSP's More Than Sad[6] content into the department's online training for educators in suicide prevention. In South Carolina, they do several suicide training institutes throughout the year where they bring mental health professionals from each school or from each district to one central location. The institute is a train-the-trainer model, so each person goes back to their school or district and trains additional personnel.

Both of those are done in partnership with the state department of education. Utah has sustained investment in putting together infrastructure within the state to support suicide prevention broadly and also within the schools. They have dedicated state positions for coordinators of state suicide prevention and school suicide prevention that work together.

AFSP is working collaboratively with other suicide prevention and mental health organizations to come up with more tools to measure success and work with state officials to start employing people who are dedicated to this area. As the data comes out of the National Violent Death Reporting System (NVDRS), researchers will start building on that to figure out what's working.

Concurrently with all these changes in policy, public awareness campaigns about suicide have increased. The public is more aware, and people are talking about it. So some of the increases in the suicide rate may be due to its being recognized more. It's just hard to put something that didn't happen into numbers.

Recommendations for Initiating a Suicide Prevention Program in a School or District

With AFSP chapters in all fifty states, any individual, school, or community group can reach out to their local chapter to request assistance. AFSP has developed evidence-based educational programs for school personnel, for students, and for parents. The *Model School District Policy* is free and available to all schools and districts.

A local AFSP chapter can serve as a catalyst for schools. After taking stock of existing programs and policies, they'll suggest improvements. The chapters can provide speakers and may have the financial means to offer materials at little or no cost.

AFSP works with various groups that offer other quality programs. Safe-TALK or ASIST Training from LivingWorks Education and Mental Health First Aid training from the National Council for Behavioral Health are available in many communities through local AFSP chapters. For more resources, schools can contact the Jason Foundation, one of the organizations dedicated to high school programs, or the Jed Foundation, which focuses on suicide prevention within colleges and universities. The Trevor Project works with LGBTQ stakeholders. Also, the Suicide Prevention Resource Center (SPRC) hosts a website that lists all of the suicide prevention coordinators for each state. Schools are encouraged to make contact to find out what resources are available locally.

The hardest part of starting a suicide prevention program is knowing where to begin. With so many resources available, it's just a matter of seeking out the information and taking action.[7]

BASIC COMPONENTS OF A SUICIDE PREVENTION MODEL FOR SCHOOLS

Suicide prevention is part of school safety. It should be included in a school's crisis/emergency plan or as a stand-alone policy. All staff members should be familiar with clearly written policies and procedures. Three main components form the framework of a comprehensive prevention plan: prevention, intervention, and postvention.

Prevention starts with knowing how to identify students at risk and referring them to a professional for help. While teachers are by nature caring and nurturing, they need specific training to recognize signs of mental health conditions and suicide risk. School districts should include annual prevention training in their policies even if state law doesn't require it.

Prevention is a group effort. Educators must talk openly about suicide signs and prevention just as they would discuss any other issue that affects their students' academic and social growth. It's normal for schools to hold regular meetings to discuss interventions for students who are struggling. Problems might revolve around academic subjects like reading, math, or language, or they could concern health or behavior problems. Why not consider interventions for students at risk of harming themselves?

The prospect of *intervention* can intimidate educators. Teachers aren't trained counselors and are not sure what to do if a student is at high risk or attempts suicide at school. With a comprehensive intervention policy in place, all staff will know how to intervene and get help for their students.

Postvention is about the response to a suicide death in the school community. Because it's so sudden and unexpected, the loss is devastating and shifts the entire school's focus. Having a plan in place before a crisis means the difference between chaos and control. Schools will be better prepared to respond and avoid suicide contagion. Teachers can provide support to students, parents, and each other. Comprehensive postvention policies not only help schools recover from a suicide loss but also bolster future prevention efforts.

A TRAGIC SCENARIO

Without any training in suicide prevention, schools make mistakes that can affect the lives of survivors of a suicide loss forever. No one ever expects a suicide to happen in their school community, so when it does, not everyone knows how to respond. Too often, students find out about a death through social media before school staff learn of it through the grapevine. In their efforts to control reactions, district officials inform the school staff not to speak of it. Talk of the death shuts down and offers of assistance are turned away. Imagine the emotional turmoil that will affect that district in the aftermath and for years following the tragedy.

The scenario could turn out differently. If the district's emergency plan included a suicide prevention policy, administrators and teachers would know how to respond. By acknowledging the loss, they show respect to the person who has died. Talking about the tragedy leads to an opportunity to teach the school community about the causes and prevention of suicide and helps survivors process their feelings and recover.

LEGISLATING TO PREVENT SUICIDE

Advocates work with state governments around the country to educate legislators about mental health and suicide prevention. Some states have already passed legislation that requires training for educators and mandates prevention policies. Others have taken first steps, passing laws that allow teachers to earn recertification credit hours for taking suicide prevention or mental health first aid training. Any action that helps increase awareness is worthwhile.

Ten states currently mandate suicide prevention training for school personnel. Laws vary, but most range from requiring one or two hours of training every year through self-study or in-service programs. Some require training only for high school teachers, administrators, and counselors while others include training for all school personnel. Texas laws go beyond the minimum to require classes in mental health, substance abuse, and youth suicide for teacher certification.

Seventeen other states and Washington, DC, require training only once, or every five years during a typical recertification cycle. Most specify one or two hours, although Wyoming, a state with one of the highest suicide rates in the country, requires eight hours every four years for teachers and administrators.

Fifteen states have legislation in place that encourages training for school personnel by allowing recertification credit hours, but they avoid mandating the training.

Twelve states plus DC require school suicide prevention, intervention, and postvention programming and eight states encourage schools to have prevention policies in place. Others have suicide prevention statutes limited to specific requirements regarding parent notification or offering parent seminars.

The American Foundation for Suicide Prevention (AFSP) recommends mandating training for school personnel and adopting comprehensive school policies. Through collaboration with the Jason Flatt Foundation and the help of local volunteers meeting with their state legislators, many of the states that have already passed legislation adopted the Jason Flatt Act, a bill mandating two hours of suicide prevention training for school personnel. Legislators included their own variations to meet the needs of each individual state.

To promote advocacy work in states where the Jason Flatt Act has not yet been introduced, AFSP developed model legislation for local volunteers. The model provides a place to start for people interested in beginning the process of passing legislation for suicide prevention in schools.

WHERE TO FIND SUICIDE PREVENTION TRAINING

One goal of the 2012 National Strategy for Suicide Prevention (NSSP) is for all states to have a prevention plan in place. Every plan should include detailed goals for suicide prevention training in schools. School and district leaders will find contact information for all states and U.S. territories on the Suicide Prevention Resource Center (SPRC) website. Local suicide prevention organizations offer free training for schools and community organizations.

There are plenty of resources available. If training is not accessible locally, suicide prevention organizations and federal agencies offer access to free programs on their websites. The brief list below suggests a starting place for schools interested in finding effective evidence-based prevention programs:

SPRC: Suicide Prevention Resource Center[8]

AAS: American Association of Suicidology[9]
AFSP: American Foundation for Suicide Prevention[10]

SUICIDE PREVENTION TRAINING PROGRAMS AND RESOURCES FOR SCHOOLS

This list summarizes training programs often used by schools. But there are many other quality programs available. Most training is free, although some providers may charge a fee.

- *Mental Health First Aid*[11] training is recommended for at least two people on each campus. This training is available nationwide and teaches participants how to identify, understand, and respond to signs of mental illnesses and substance abuse disorders in their communities.
- Training in *safeTALK*[12] is for everyone willing to participate. This half-day program teaches participants to recognize and engage persons who might have thoughts of suicide and to connect them with community resources trained in suicide intervention.
- *Applied Suicide Intervention Skills Training (ASIST)*[13] is a two-day, two-trainer workshop designed for anyone who may be the first to talk with a person at risk, but has little or no training. ASIST can also provide those in formal helping roles with professional development in suicide first aid.
- Training on recognizing signs of depression for students, staff, and parents is most effective if done every year. Examples of programs available include *Signs of Suicide*,[14] *More Than Sad*,[15] and *Signs Matter: Early Detection*.[16]
- The Jason Flatt Foundation offers several courses designed to meet recertification requirements. They recommend starting with *Youth Suicide: A Silent Epidemic*,[17] an online self-paced training module. It's an introduction to the national health issue of youth suicide and provides information about warning signs and elevated risk factors, and it offers other important supporting materials.
- *QPR (Question, Persuade, and Refer) Gatekeeper Training for Suicide Prevention*[18] is a short educational program designed to teach lay and professional "gatekeepers" the warning signs of a suicide crisis and how to respond.
- *Kognito At-Risk for PK–12 Educators*,[19] is a one-hour, online, interactive gatekeeper training program that teaches educators to recognize and respond to signs of psychological distress in students.
- *LEADS: For Youth (Linking Education and Awareness of Depression and Suicide)*[20] is a high school curriculum designed to increase knowledge of

depression and suicide and to improve intentions to engage in help-seeking behaviors.

- While not specifically designed for suicide prevention, the *Good Behavior Game (GBG)*[21] is a classroom behavior management game that helps elementary school teachers reduce aggression and other behavioral problems and create a positive learning environment.
- The Suicide Prevention Resource Center (SPRC) offers several self-paced online courses useful for school staff: *Counseling on Access to Lethal Means (CALM), A Strategic Planning Approach to Suicide Prevention,* and *Locating and Understanding Data for Suicide Prevention.*[22] Schools working with Native American youth may want additional resources that are more specific to their needs.
- *To Live to See the Great Day That Dawns: Preventing Suicide by American Indian and Alaska Native Youth and Young Adults*[23] is a manual that lays the groundwork for community-based suicide prevention and mental health promotion plans for American Indian and Alaska Native teens and young adults. It addresses risks, protective factors, and awareness and describes prevention models for action.
- The Tribal TTA Center[24] provides training and technical help to support mental health in tribal communities and honor self-determination.
- The SPRC offers several suicide prevention resources specific to American Indian/Alaska Native settings.[25]

WHY SCHOOLS DON'T ADDRESS SUICIDE PREVENTION

Despite all the information available on suicide prevention, few school districts set up suicide prevention programs if their community has never experienced a suicide loss. Barriers that inhibit progress are varied.

By far the strongest impediment is the stigma of suicide. It is such a taboo topic that school leaders in many communities hesitate to address it. There's a sense that if they talk about it, it will happen. Conversely, if suicide prevention is never mentioned, suicide may seem less likely to be a problem and is simply ignored.

With no sense of urgency, administrators may not consider suicide prevention a priority. Even if directed by state or district leaders to have a suicide prevention program, after the plan is written and approved it might never be implemented. It's likely to sit in a binder on a shelf along with all the other emergency plans.

Until it happens. When a school suffers the sudden loss of a student who has taken their own life, shock and dismay disrupts the entire community. Administrators struggle to figure out how to respond. Because of the stigma, reactions may include blame for the victim or parents. The district will dispatch teams of counselors to provide support at the time of the crisis, but staff members often feel an enduring sense of guilt for overlooking signs or not preventing the death. Finger-pointing and confusion linger, limiting the school's ability to recover.

The other insurmountable obstacle is time. To implement an effective prevention program, time has to be built into the daily schedule to provide training to administrators, teachers and staff, students, and parents. Not just once, but every year. If it isn't a part of the school culture, a program the school community identifies with and will always maintain, then it will never be truly effective.

JUST DO IT

With creative planning, all K–12 schools can integrate suicide prevention programming for students into the curriculum. K–6 schools may choose health classes to teach about mental health using age-appropriate materials, while middle and high schools might include it in English, science, or physical education classes to be sure to reach all students. Because of the emphasis on high-stakes test scores, schools tend to prioritize subjects assessed on standardized tests. Mental health is not one of them; however, it is equally important.

Laws addressing suicide prevention training vary widely. Teachers and staff can receive training in suicide prevention during staff meetings, scheduled professional development days, or on their own time. Some states encourage educators to become informed about suicide prevention by taking mental health and suicide prevention courses for recertification credit. Others mandate training, requiring at least two hours per year. A close look at state statutes reveals a broad range of expectations for schools ranging from a mention of suicide prevention and a suggestion that teachers could choose to participate in training to a comprehensive policy encompassing prevention, intervention, and postvention.

BEYOND POLICIES AND PROCEDURES

In a school that has established a culture of caring, everybody in the school is part of the plan. They look out for each other. School leaders engage the whole school community in building a positive climate and creating a safe environment where students are willing to share their feelings with others.

By showing they care, school leaders set the tone. Their role is to inspire the school community to work toward a common goal. Teachers, instructional assistants, students, parents, nurses, counselors, psychologists, specialists, cafeteria workers, office staff, custodians, and administrators form a power-ful force together.

Because it can be uncomfortable to get involved with emotional situa-tions, it's easier to ignore signs of distress in students than to address them. So instead of turning a blind eye to those who struggle or seem isolated, students and staff must learn to ask the right questions. When it becomes normal to pay attention to others in need of help, the result is a safer environ-ment.

Learning how to help students or colleagues struggling with depression empowers teachers and staff to take action. In times of crisis, knowing what to do will save lives. Within a culture of caring, taking time to develop and implement a comprehensive suicide prevention plan is a logical extension of what is already in place.

THE FUTURE OF SUICIDE PREVENTION IN SCHOOLS

As more schools and districts recognize the urgent need for suicide preven-tion plans, it's important to avoid jumping on the bandwagon without careful planning. To throw together some ideas and call it a plan just to keep up with the neighbors isn't enough. Contact experts in suicide prevention or use the resources listed in this book to make sure you do it the right way. To find current examples of what other states and districts across the country are doing, visit the Suicide Prevention Resource Center's website.[26]

PREVENTION VERSUS CRISIS INTERVENTION

More progress has been made in suicide prevention in the last twenty years than ever before. No single approach will adequately address the problem though. It is in our best interest to learn and collaborate, access any resources available in a community, and keep the conversation going.

We have come a long way since the concept of suicide prevention first emerged and have learned much about how to prevent suicide before a crisis occurs. But to actually reduce suicide rates, every person, school, district, community, tribe, and state government must commit to active participation. Schools are on the front lines and need to take responsible action.

By being proactive, we can save lives. Think about it—wouldn't it make sense that along with hiring a lifeguard to save a drowning victim at the beach we should teach everyone to swim so we can prevent the drowning before it happens?

Chapter Three

Changing the Mindset

Suicide happens to other people. It's not part of our lives; it's not taking up space in our heads. Why try to prevent something that isn't a problem in our school? Educators have enough to do without taking time to prepare for something that won't happen.

There's truth in the saying "You don't know what you don't know." Not being exposed to something doesn't mean it isn't happening. Learning that suicide is the second leading cause of death for youth ages ten to twenty-four shocks teachers. But it starts to make sense that 90 percent of people who die by suicide have a mental illness, often undiagnosed and untreated. Statistics telling such a tragic story make it harder to ignore.

Even with that knowledge, it's difficult to initiate an uncomfortable and time-consuming project when people don't want to talk about it and don't see the need. It's one of those things that maybe we should do something about, but we don't want to, so we let it go. In states where suicide prevention training is mandated it can seem like just another hoop teachers feel they have to jump through to keep their jobs.

So how do we change our mindset? It starts with changing our perception. Have you ever thought of trying to improve your health by getting more exercise and eating healthy foods? Why bother? Because we've learned that we can prevent heart attacks by choosing a heart-healthy diet. Increasing physical activity and avoiding certain foods reduces cholesterol. We can even lower blood pressure by including meditation in daily routines. Taking action prevents potential problems from occurring.

If we can prevent problems in our physical health, doesn't it make sense to do the same for mental health? Learning to choose healthy foods starts in preschool or kindergarten when teachers encourage children to eat fruits and vegetables. All students take physical education classes because schools want students to know the importance of physical activity. Is there any reason we shouldn't teach about mental health at an early age too?

When you think about it, there is no need to separate physical health and mental health, or mental illness and physical illness. The problem lies in deeply rooted cultural attitudes about mental illness. People fear what they don't understand even if they rarely admit that they fear mental illness for that very reason.

Mental illness is the leading cause of suicide death. We need to think about teaching prevention for mental illness early on. Just like any physical disease, with early diagnosis and treatment, we can prevent death caused by mental illness. To change the current mindset, people need to talk about suicide and learn to be preventative in the same way that we recognize heart-healthy diets prevent heart attacks. In our society, there is a deeply ingrained fear of disclosing mental illness because of ridicule, job loss, and mistaken perception that it's a weakness rather than an illness. The pervasive attitude is that we should just get over it. Why isn't it the same with cancer, diabetes, heart disease, or even allergies? By changing our own mindsets, we can help to stop the stigma.

Look at what's happened with breast cancer research. Not so many years ago, people were embarrassed to use the word "breast" in public. In recent years, however, businesses have jumped on the bandwagon to join the cause, and it seems like almost every brand flaunts the ubiquitous pink ribbons. Because public awareness has exploded, and research has been well funded, we are winning the battle. Women are surviving at much higher rates than ever before. There is hope that we can overcome breast cancer.

What if we could create the same intensity for suicide prevention as for breast cancer research? Well-known statistics indicate that one out of every eight women will get breast cancer.[1] Yet one in five adults experiences mental illness in a year, and one in twenty-five adults experiences a serious mental illness each year that substantially interferes with or limits one or more major life activities. One in five children aged thirteen to eighteen experiences a severe mental disorder at some point during their life.[2] We need to talk about that!

Creating a culture of caring means we notice others when they are suffering and offer help instead of averting our eyes and walking by. Or we understand that misbehavior is often a cry for help, so instead of punishing students for their actions, we take time to dig a little deeper and find out the cause of the behavior. We teach young children to tell an adult when they have a problem. We need to make it normal for students to ask for help not only when they have a stomachache but also if their brains feel bad.

EXPERT COMMENTARY: LEO HART, SCHOOL COUNSELOR,
VALLEY HIGH SCHOOL, SUNNY VALLEY, ARIZONA

Valley High School serves just over two thousand students in a rural suburb in Arizona. The school's motto, "Excellent Achievement in a Caring Environment," sets the tone for a culture of caring.

Having suffered five teen suicides in two years, the school community urgently needed to recover and prevent further tragedies. Counselor Leo Hart, with a background in crisis counseling, felt strongly that students, teachers, and parents needed to learn about suicide causes and prevention.

With the support of his school district, Leo helped bring the Signs of Suicide (SOS) program to Valley High School.

Postvention Leads to Prevention

> "Unfortunately, we had multiple student suicides. We really needed more support, more help."

No school expects to experience suicide loss on their campus. When it happens, it affects the lives of every member of the school community.

During his first year at Valley High School, Leo noticed that more and more students were coming to the counseling office with mental health issues like anxiety and depression. Because of the recent student suicides, he knew the school needed more support. When he reached out to EMPACT Suicide Prevention Center, the local suicide prevention agency, he learned about the Signs of Suicide (SOS)[3] program and thought it would be a great program to implement in the school.

Schools feel like they're getting kind of pinched in different areas for in-class time, and at first students and teachers were really hesitant. There was a little bit of pushback about taking class time away from teachers, with everything that's expected of them these days. Overall, though, it's such an important program to implement because there are so many different things that students can gain from it. All schools should do it.

Everyone in the counseling department sees the importance of it, and all of the principals, assistant principals, and superintendents in our district see the value of SOS as a suicide prevention program. They'll make sure that we continue the program in the future.

Getting Buy-In from Staff

We got hit pretty hard. It's been a tough stretch for suicides, so more education and more informative presentations on these topics were definitely in high demand. When administrators found out about the SOS program, that it was actually free and given by mental health experts in this area, they were on board pretty much immediately.

From a counseling perspective, since it came from principals down to the teachers, it was really easy to schedule with those teachers. They knew when it was going to happen, the dates, and that it was going to go through the English department. For most schools, English is the easiest class to go through, just because all students are required to take it for graduation.

The first year we did every grade level, and this year we're doing just freshmen and seniors. We also implemented the SOS program in eighth grade at some of our middle schools. The district's on board to start the SOS program at an even younger age, going down to fifth and sixth grade. If it's a prevention program, it should start earlier, way before high school.

Even if they have never had a suicide, every school should be prepared. The SOS program is not just about suicide prevention. It addresses issues that all schools are facing—bullying, substance abuse, peer pressure, depression, and anxiety. The program is free for schools, and the student presentations will take up only one class period. It's worth the time.

Getting Buy-In from Students

"We're trying to get the message to students that if they're worried about themselves or their peers, they really need to talk with a trusted adult so we can connect them with the help that they need."

The students have reacted really well to the SOS program. We compiled some data and found that last year 9 percent of the freshman students marked on the screener form that they wanted to talk with a counselor, or they were worried about themselves or a peer. This year, we had 12 percent, so there was an increase in students who wanted to talk with a counselor about a concern they had about themselves or someone else. It's great that the kids are feeling more comfortable and more responsible about coming to talk with a trusted adult because that's pretty much what it's all about.

Getting Buy-In from Parents

"Parents were really pushing for the school to do something."

Parents have been part of the conversation too. They were really pushing for the school to do something, but it's not just the school. It's parents, it's the community, and it's the school. We're all in this together. We all have to work together to help these kids. Providing the SOS program for all of our students is just one thing that the school is doing.

If students mark on the assessment after the SOS presentation that they are struggling with depression or suicidal thoughts, we make calls home to the parents. We tell them the EMPACT team recommended outpatient counseling for their son or daughter, or it could be another recommendation. It just depends on the case. We ask the kids if they are interested in the group counseling offered by the school. If they agree, we can offer that as additional support when we call their parents.

Group counseling is another thing we've started on our campus. There was a need for students to have the opportunity to share things that they're going through with others and come up with ways they can improve their situations. About forty or fifty students get counseling each year. That's one other thing that we can do to help.

We've seen a positive transition away from the stigma of suicide in our community. There's that myth, "The more you talk about suicide, the more it happens." We've been getting the message across that the more you talk about it, that's more support that you're giving people, whether they're students or community members or parents. It's becoming the norm that people are more willing to talk openly about it. You can see that in our data too, with the increase in freshmen coming to the counseling office wanting to talk.

School Counselors Help Support Student Mental Health

The American School Counselor Association (ASCA) suggested a ratio for students of 250 to 1, but we're at around 550. Yes, we need more staff. Class sizes are pretty big too, so more teachers would be great as well. As far as the group counseling goes, there are hardly any high schools in the area that actually run group counseling on a regular basis, but we really try to squeeze time to provide that for our students.

For any type of school counseling license or degree, there are classes on mental health, but it's mostly geared toward academic advising. Additional training is always good for counselors and teachers too. We've had mental health training for all of our staff members, looking at warning signs and protocols, how to talk with students if they're feeling down, and making sure we connect the kids to the counseling department. We're going to see more of that.

Advice on Starting a Suicide Prevention Program

"When you look at the numbers, it's obvious that our state, even our whole country, needs more education and more information on mental health and suicide prevention."

Don't try to do it alone. School counselors are very pressed for time, and it's tough to find additional time to implement a new program. Have the mental health experts come in and present. Pick up the phone and call the local suicide prevention agency. EMPACT made it really easy to get the program started. They were very transparent with all the paperwork going home to parents and what they would be presenting. They have a fine-tuned process that's very easy to explain to administrators, teachers, and all staff.

With good planning and communication before rollout, any school can start a comprehensive suicide prevention program.

Note: Names have been changed to protect the privacy of the school district and staff.

GET THE CONVERSATION STARTED

Prevention starts with awareness. To get the conversation started, invite a speaker to come in to talk to your staff about suicide prevention in schools. Arming teachers with basic information about what to look for in their students and what to do about it empowers them to take action and refer students for help.

Depression is by far the most common form of mental illness. With training and awareness, teachers, students, and other members of the school community can learn to recognize the signs. And take action to address the needs of any student who suffers from it. Students with suicidal thoughts often give signals of their intentions. If students talk about wanting to kill themselves, write about being deeply depressed or sad, or believe they have no reason to live—take it seriously.

It is an unfortunate myth that talking with someone about their suicidal thoughts will cause the person suffering to follow through with it. The opposite is true. Anyone who talks about suicide, even if only in veiled messages, wants someone else to know about it. Although they may not ask for help directly, they are delivering a message. A caring educator can start a conversation by simply asking the student, "Are you thinking about hurting yourself?"

In middle and high school students, the signs of depression are often nonverbal and look like typical teenage behavior. A lot of teens sleep too much or not enough. But when these behaviors last for several weeks or months, chances are there are deeper issues at play. Moods and attitudes change when a person is severely depressed. Young people may seem more irritable or gloomy or display uncharacteristic rage or anxiety. Withdrawing from usual activities, excessive use of alcohol or drugs, giving away possessions, or displaying nontypical behavior are all associated with thoughts of suicide.

Students often notice peers who are struggling with depression long before adults catch on. Teens rarely know what to do with their knowledge, though, and hide it from adults. It's important to talk to students about why they must not keep depression or suicidal thoughts a secret. Encourage students to get help by talking to a trusted adult, such as a teacher, school counselor, or nurse.

Pay attention to the signs. When a student expresses a sense of deep sadness or despair, never tell them to "just get over it" or "give it time, things will get better." For people who have never experienced real depression, it's difficult to identify the feelings the sufferer is going through or how much mental pain they are in. If you see the warning signs, don't wonder about it—act. Refer the student to the school psychologist or counselor if available. If not, the school nurse can help. They will contact parents and assist them with a referral to the appropriate mental health service provider.

STOP THE STIGMA

People who suffer from depression are often ashamed of their illness. They feel too embarrassed to let others know they are struggling with mental illness because of the stigma associated with it. It is up to all of us to recognize the signs. Normalize reaching out to help people with mental illness. Fight the stigma by speaking up. Suicide can be prevented by addressing the underlying causes.

People refer to the act of suicide as if it were a crime, saying that someone has "committed" suicide. If a person dies from a heart attack, no one ever says they committed a heart attack. Suicide is no different. It results from a long illness. Lacking a cure, a person suffering from severe depression is in so much pain that death seems the only way to end it.

We need to stop saying that a person "commits" suicide. They die by suicide or from a mental illness. We can help eliminate the stigma by treating a death by suicide as the end of an illness rather than an act of cowardice or a crime.

If a school is touched by the suicide death of a student or staff member, administrators should not try to hush it up. With the family's permission, inform the school community about the death. By sharing the facts along with information about support available for students, administrators educate students and parents without judgment. Teaching the warning signs of suicidal behavior and providing a list of resources available in the community helps healing and recovery begin.

Because of the stigma, suicides often go unreported and the deaths are listed as accidents or the result of some other illness. Ignoring the issue limits the ability of communities to heal by talking openly about what happened.

Inaccurate reporting prevents researchers of suicide prevention from collecting actionable data that may help them find better solutions.

KNOWLEDGE IS POWER

Learning about suicide and how to prevent a problem gives us the power to change our attitudes and behavior. The Suicide Prevention Resource Center (SPRC) promotes a comprehensive approach to suicide prevention.[4] This list has been adapted for school settings.

1. Identify and assist persons at risk: When people are depressed or struggling with suicidal thoughts, they rarely seek help on their own. Recognizing warning signs and knowing how to get help are the first steps. Schools can provide gatekeeper training for staff and use basic suicide screening tools with students.
2. Increase help-seeking: Teach people to recognize when they need support and help them find it. Publish self-help tools and run outreach campaigns as a regular annual event at schools. Make it the cultural norm for people to ask for help and know how to find it.
3. Ensure access to effective mental health and suicide care and treatment: Access to evidence-based treatments, interventions, and coordinated systems of care is essential. Schools need to have knowledge about mental health services available in their communities and notify parents.
4. Support safe care transitions and create organizational linkages: Communication between organizations providing care for at-risk students, parents, and school mental health professionals is essential.
5. Respond efficiently to individuals in crisis: Schools need to know how to access a range of services beyond publishing hotline or helpline contact information. Risk-assessment tools can help guide decisions about the level of care needed—from peer-support programs to calling a mobile crisis team or hospital-based psychiatric emergency services.
6. Provide immediate and long-term postvention: Having a plan in place to respond effectively and compassionately to a suicide death allows schools to respond immediately and focus on those affected by a suicide death. Postvention efforts should also include intermediate and long-term supports for people bereaved by suicide.
7. Reduce access to means of suicide: Educate the school community—families and students—on how to reduce access to lethal means of self-harm. Safely storing medications and firearms can reduce the risk of death by suicide.

8. Enhance life skills and resilience: Help people build life skills such as critical thinking, stress management, and coping. Resilience—the ability to cope with adversity and adapt to change—is a protective factor against suicide risk. Teach ways to develop optimism, positive self-concept, and hope.
9. Promote social connectedness and support: Create a culture of caring by building programs that offer activities to reduce isolation, promote a sense of belonging, and foster emotionally supportive relationships.

THE MINDSET AT OUR SCHOOL IS POSITIVE SO THERE IS NO NEED TO CHANGE IT

If you identify positively with your school community and feel a sense of belonging, you want it to stay that way. It is normal that when we feel comfortable within our work setting, and there are no obvious problems, there is complacency. Why change anything if we're all getting along just fine? If you look more closely, however, there is a high probability that there are students at your school who are struggling with serious problems that are not being addressed. Don't wait for a crisis to create change.

Consider the data available from the Centers for Disease Control and Prevention (CDC) collected from the Youth Risk Behavior Survey. The national Youth Risk Behavior Survey (YRBS) monitors health behaviors that contribute to the leading causes of death, disability, and social problems among youth and adults in the United States. The survey is conducted every two years during the spring semester and provides data representative of ninth- through twelfth-grade students in public and private schools throughout the United States. If we focus on the results related to suicide risk, the responses are disturbing.

The YRBS asks four questions about suicide.

1. Have you felt sad or hopeless almost every day in a row for two or more weeks so that it affected your usual activities in the past twelve months? (1 out of 4 students)
2. Have you seriously considered suicide in the past twelve months? (1 out of 6)
3. Have you made a plan about how to commit suicide in the past twelve months? (1 out of 7)
4. Have you attempted suicide one or more times in the past twelve months? (1 out of 13)

Based on results of the Youth Risk Behavior Survey, current trends predict that in the next twelve months

- 6.6 million youth will begin experiencing symptoms of clinical depression
- 3.7 million youth will seriously consider suicide
- 3 million youth will make a plan
- 1.76 million, an average of 4,840 youth per day, will make an attempt[5]

Classroom teachers can make the numbers more real by applying them to the students they know and teach every day. In an average class of thirty students, the results from the survey questions are more personal and alarming.

1. Have you felt sad or hopeless almost every day in a row for two or more weeks so that it affected your usual activities in the past twelve months? (7 or 8 of your students)
2. Have you seriously considered suicide in the past twelve months? (5 of your students)
3. Have you made a plan about how to commit suicide in the past twelve months? (4 of your students)
4. Have you attempted suicide one or more times in the past twelve months? (2 or 3 of your students)

HOW A CULTURE OF CARING LED TO CRISIS SUPPORT

DoSomething.org is an organization for getting teens involved in community service projects. Created for today's youth, they maintain all communication through texting. They started out by doing service activities for local communities like collecting food for food banks, writing cards for senior citizens, and delivering basic hygiene supplies to homeless shelters. But along with messages from young people offering to pitch it, the text line often got messages asking for help.

Because of those messages, organizers created Crisis Text Line.[6] It was first launched in Chicago and El Paso. Within four months it expanded to all 240 area codes in the United States. Anyone who sends a text message to 741741 will get a response from a volunteer counselor trained to help people in pain.

Thirty percent of the text messages are about suicide and depression. Not just a suicide line, Crisis Text Line wants to make it easier for anyone in pain to get help. Counselors take texters from a heated moment to a cool calm. If a texter is unwilling to come up with a safety plan, active rescue is initiated and emergency services are called.

Most schools will not create their own text lines to support at-risk students, but the reason for including this story is to emphasize that many ordinary teens who seem to be quite normally adjusted may be suffering from depression or suicidal thoughts and don't know what to do about it. In a school environment where staff and students notice others who may be suffering, becoming more aware of signs and risk factors helps educators know how to respond and take action.

SCHOOL WEBSITE RESOURCES

Feeling super stressed? Worried about a friend's mental health—or your own? Get tips to help manage your emotions and see what to do if you are in crisis.

Are there any resources for suicide prevention on your school's website? There should be. As awareness grows, schools can provide support to the school community by posting information and resources about student safety and wellness. Make it accessible for students, parents, and staff. A list of community resources is important, but a proactive school district will include a webpage designed specifically for students seeking help.

An excellent example any district can use as a model is Fairfax County Public Schools in Virginia.[7] Immediately visible after clicking on the Student Wellness Tips and Strategies link on the home page is a bold message that engages students: "Feeling super stressed? Worried about a friend's mental health—or your own? Get tips to help manage your emotions and see what to do if you are in crisis. Remember, help is just a text, click, or call away! If you are in crisis, text NEEDHELP to 85511, call 1-800-273-TALK, or dial 911."

As visitors to the site scroll down, they find multiple links to specific topics relevant to teens. The site includes video clips about the Crisis Text Line and mental health, resources on how to help a friend in crisis, and how to handle peer pressure. Tips to ease test anxiety, getting through the loss of a friend or loved one, and a well-written explanation of *13 Reasons Why* address common teen issues.

As awareness about teen suicide grows, more districts are adding safety and wellness resources for students to their websites. Because young people are far more likely to interact with well-designed web content than to scroll through a lengthy document listing community resources, it is worthwhile.

A school district web page with high student traffic is useful for promoting special events. For example, student clubs can showcase multiple activities during Suicide Prevention Month in September. Interactive information booths, student performances, fundraisers, and suicide awareness campus walks increase engagement and integrate suicide prevention into the school's culture.

FIREARMS AND SUICIDE

Many students come from families that view guns as part of their way of life. Guns are present in their homes. So as the gun control debate rages on in our country, it is important to understand the relationship between firearms and suicide prevention. After the school shooting in Parkland, Florida, the American Association of Suicidology (AAS) issued a statement about the role of firearms in suicide. Highlighting the relationship between restricting access to firearms and reducing suicide deaths serves as a reminder to parents. Means safety, or limiting access to lethal means, is a proven method of suicide prevention.

Regardless of your feelings about the right to own guns, you should know that half of all suicide deaths in the United States, over 22,000 in 2015, resulted from self-inflicted gunshot wounds. Experts estimate that 85 to 95 percent of all suicide attempts using firearms are successful. In comparison, only 2 to 3 percent of attempters die by intentional overdose—the most commonly used method.[8] Even though firearm access does not cause suicidal ideation, it increases suicide risk among all members of a home when the firearms are stored unlocked and loaded.

Suicide prevention experts have collaborated in recent years with providers of firearms to educate communities about restricting access. Gun owners take a proactive role in suicide prevention by making lethal weapons inaccessible. They help change the culture and save lives.

WHO ARE SUICIDE PREVENTION ADVOCATES?

You are. Talking with others about suicide prevention makes a difference. Most people know little about it. If you feel passionate about the issue, get more involved by talking to school and district leaders. Find out what the status of suicide prevention is in your district. Attend a school board meeting and explain how training teachers, staff, and students increases awareness.

Find out if your state has legislation in place requiring mental health or suicide prevention training for teachers. If not, talk to legislators and government officials about supporting mental health and suicide prevention. Advocacy at the state level is not hard, it just takes participation.

Some states allocate funding to hire an expert to monitor prevention training across the state. Yours may have someone who can help. If not, check the SPRC website for the name of the person listed as your state point of contact.[9] Starting a suicide prevention plan in your school could be just a few phone calls or email messages away.

WE ARE ALL RESPONSIBLE

We are all responsible for the safety of our students. Preventing suicide is part of that. We cannot allow fear and stigma to get in the way of creating an environment where it's normal to talk openly about feelings, sadness, grief, hopelessness, mental illness, and suicide. And where it is normal to seek or offer help. There is no excuse for not taking steps to prevent tragedy and save lives.

Chapter Four

Prevention

"Stop, drop, and roll" is a simple fire safety technique taught to school children so they know what to do in case they get caught in a house fire. It works. It's simple and easy to remember. We take time to teach it because being prepared can save lives.

We make emergency plans and hope we never have to use them. If we do, knowing what to do in times of crisis helps prevent chaos and gives us a sense of control. Most schools have an emergency or crisis plan. Every school practices fire drills and lockdowns and many hold active shooter drills. But suicide prevention plans are relatively rare.

A wise school leader recognizes that a suicide prevention plan is an important part of school safety. Teachers and staff trained to recognize risk factors and warning signs of suicidal thinking know how to prevent suicide. They learn to safely intervene with a student in crisis. If a suicide death occurs in the school community, they are prepared to respond appropriately.

Because a suicide prevention plan is more complex than other safety plans, developing one may seem overwhelming. Fortunately, there is no need to reinvent the wheel. Several states have already created comprehensive suicide prevention policies, plans, and toolkits for schools. Find examples in chapter 10, under resources.

If your school district is in a state that doesn't mandate suicide prevention or provide policies, you'll find that the *Model School District Policy on Suicide Prevention*[1] serves as a solid foundation. It suggests model language to help schools create their own policies and includes explanations, commentary, and resources.

The American Foundation for Suicide Prevention (AFSP) developed the Model Policy in collaboration with the Trevor Project, the National Association of School Psychologists (NASP), and the American School Counselor

Association (ASCA). Based on best practices described in the *Suicide Prevention Toolkit for High Schools* published by SAMHSA in 2012 and encompassing existing laws, the Model Policy is a practical guide for school districts.

EXPERT COMMENTARY: JILL COOK, ASSISTANT DIRECTOR, AMERICAN SCHOOL COUNSELOR ASSOCIATION

The American School Counselor Association (ASCA) provides resources, professional development, and support to school counselors. With a strong background in teaching, administration, and school counseling, Jill Cook helped develop two award programs: the Recognized ASCA Model Program that recognizes exemplary comprehensive school counseling programs based on the *ASCA National Model: A Framework for School Counseling Programs* and the School Counselor of the Year program. She works with collaborative partner organizations to advance the modern role of the school counselor.

The Critical Need for School-Based Mental Health Professionals

Schools need adequate staffing to include school counselors, school psychologists, school social workers, and school nurses to help address student mental health concerns. Most states have a mandate for school counselors, although many are unfunded.

School-based mental health professionals should be part of the school and district crisis planning process. If there are no school-based mental health staff members at a school, then administrators must partner and work with community organizations to ensure that students get the services they need when there are mental health concerns.

It's equally important to provide training in suicide prevention to school staff. Not just teachers in the classroom, but anyone who works with students—custodians, bus drivers, coaches, administrators, and all support staff. Staff members should understand what the warning signs may be, know the process to follow if there are concerns about a student, and notify the designated person who will take the next steps.

EVOLUTION OF THE SCHOOL COUNSELORS' ROLE

"School counselors and school counseling departments should be planning, delivering, implementing, and evaluating a comprehensive school counseling program that addresses students' academic, social and emotional, and career development needs."

The profession has undergone a dramatic shift in the last twenty years. School counselors are no longer just guidance counselors[2] but work with all students. They aren't limited to working with just a few through comprehensive programs. The profession has moved from being reactive and ancillary to being proactive and critical to supporting student success. School counselors deliver the comprehensive program through core curriculum classroom guidance, small groups, and individual student planning and counseling. The development of a comprehensive school counseling program should begin by looking at school and student data specifically around attendance, achievement, and behavior to determine what the school and student needs are.

ASCA has published a framework[3] for school counseling programs that clearly outlines how to develop an effective, comprehensive school counseling program. With an ideal ratio of 1:250, school counselors should spend 80 percent of their time providing direct or indirect services to students.

Focus on Prevention

> "When school counselors take on advocacy by collecting data to show impact and results, over time there is a shift. Administrators are able to see what school counselors can do. They want to be able to use that knowledge and expertise effectively."

The reality is that in schools and districts with limited resources, counselors are expected to serve many students. They often spend time on scheduling or other administrative tasks, limiting time available for counseling individuals or small groups, classroom lessons, and other services that directly or indirectly support students.

To advocate for systemic change, counselors need to build a strong relationship with their administrators. Part of the ASCA National Model is an annual collaborative agreement with administrators that defines how school counselors spend their time. Collecting data that shows impact and results goes a long way toward convincing principals they can make a difference for students. As educators with an expertise in and understanding of mental health concerns, school counselors use their knowledge and expertise most effectively by delivering services their students need.

Being involved with all students helps school counselors create a supportive environment. Getting to know them individually and being more visible puts counselors in a better position to recognize when a young person may be struggling. And it becomes more likely other students will report concerns or rumors about their peers. If counselors identify behavioral and social/emotional signs of suicide risk among their students, they will take action and get help right away. Obligated to notify parents of any concerns, counselors also need to inform the principal, teachers, and staff who work directly with a student if there is a suicide risk.

Because of their knowledge and skills, school counselors assume a leadership role in suicide awareness and prevention. They protect students by making sure teachers and other school staff have adequate training to identify warning signs and risk factors and know whom to report their concerns to. In their roles as school-based mental health professionals, counselors need to maintain current training themselves and be familiar with mental health resources available in the community.

Training for School Personnel

> "A school should have a process in place. Everybody in the school needs to know what it is and what to do."

The Model Policy (*Model School District Policy on Suicide Prevention*[4]) recommends that professional development specifically on suicide prevention and intervention is offered to all educators at least once a year. The school counselors, school psychologists, social workers, and nurses may need additional updates and training. These aren't decisions that school counselors should be making in isolation in a school, however. It should be part of a district plan, as many school districts already have or are putting policies and procedures in place.

Currently twenty-nine states require that all school personnel receive some kind of suicide intervention/prevention training as part of their professional development. This isn't just a siloed conversation, it's bigger at the district and state levels. There have to be plans and processes and procedures in place about how to respond when you have concerns about a student—not just as a school counselor or school psychologist, but as a school community.

Even if a school has no school-based mental health professionals, it's important to have a district process and plan in place. All school staff need to know what to do if they get wind of information about a student being at risk. It could be a teacher or the custodian who's told about the student at risk. The next step is to contact the parents. Unless there are mitigating circumstances, particularly with LGBTQ youth, it may be more prudent not to let the family or parents know. A school should have a process in place so everybody in the school knows what to do.

It's important not to hold on to that information in isolation. If there isn't a counselor, psychologist, social worker, or nurse available, staff should report concerns to the principal. The principal isn't going to counsel the student but will talk to the parents and suggest resources. If parents are not willing to get the student mental health support, the principal can make a neglect call to Child Protective Services. If it's an immediate threat, a call should be made to 911. It's all about communication. In a school community, it's everyone's job to keep students safe.

WHY EVERY SCHOOL NEEDS A POLICY ON SUICIDE PREVENTION

Because risk factors are often invisible and students don't express their feelings outwardly, educators need to learn to recognize behavioral changes that signal a youth in crisis. Current life events can trigger a sense of hopelessness, intensified by a young person's lack of problem-solving skills. But suicide risk is not only behavioral. School staff can't readily identify causes linked to biological and psychological factors or past history. They don't know if students have access to lethal means (weapons and drugs in particular) that contribute to a high-risk situation, so staff must teach students to be aware of those risks themselves.

To understand the urgency of having a suicide prevention plan in place, look at the rise in suicide rates. The statistics are shocking. While actual numbers vary from year to year, rates listed below represent data gathered by the Centers for Disease Control (CDC) and the Youth Behavioral Risk Survey (YBRS) in recent years.

Suicide deaths overall increased from 38,364 in 2010 to over 44,000 in 2015. It is the second leading cause of death for young people ages fourteen to twenty-four.[5] Suicide rates rise during adolescence and through age twenty-four. Boys are four times more likely to complete a suicide than girls—primarily because they are most likely to use firearms—although more girls attempt using other means. More than 150,000 youth aged ten to twenty-four receive medical care for self-inflicted injuries each year—thirty times the number who die by suicide. Almost 10 percent of girls and 5 percent of boys in grades nine through twelve report attempting suicide each year, with reports being two to six times more frequent among LGBTQ youth. Rates for Native American youth are 3.5 times higher than other ethnic groups. About 14 percent of high school students report seriously considering suicide and 11 percent report making a suicide plan.

The average high school is likely to experience at least three suicide attempts a year. Since students spend so much time at school, teachers are on the front lines. If they learn to identify students at risk, they can refer them to counselors to get help. Knowing how to respond gives teachers confidence when intervening with a student who may be struggling. If there is a suicide death in the school community, teachers and staff need to know how they can support their students.

The goal of a well-thought-out policy is to reduce the risk of suicide and to prevent suicide contagion if a death occurs. Designed for middle and high school settings, the Model Policy serves as a template any school or district can use. It addresses laws and requirements for prevention training of school personnel and students. It also provides recommended language or terminology schools can use in their own policies along with lists of best practices and resources.

OVERVIEW OF THE *MODEL DISTRICT POLICY ON SUICIDE PREVENTION*

As awareness increases, more districts see the need to be proactive and to develop comprehensive policies of their own. Schools across the country are adapting the guidelines detailed in the *Model School District Policy on Suicide Prevention* to fit their own student safety and wellness objectives. The Model Policy includes information and guidance useful for public, private, and charter schools and districts. Easy to read and concise, the 2019 edition updates the original version with a new layout, current statistics, and the latest research. The first section provides specific language schools will find useful as they develop their own policies. A commentary section addresses critical issues relevant to schools, followed by an implementation checklist and an expanded resource list.

Relevant topics include:

- access to school-based mental health services
- integrating parental involvement
- risk factors and protective factors
- characteristics of populations at elevated risk
- links between bullying and suicide
- how to communicate about suicide
- laws and liability

Regardless of the size of a school or district, a designated suicide prevention coordinator should be selected to serve as the first point of contact. Responsible for communication and implementation of the suicide prevention plan, the coordinator provides leadership and guidance at the district and school levels.

Professional development for all staff is a crucial component of the model. Even if your state doesn't require it, the Model Policy recommends annual training. Staff members must learn to notice warning signs and make referrals. All mental health professionals—school counselors, psychologists, social workers, and nurses—need additional training in prevention and crisis intervention strategies.

The Model Policy also suggests ways to include suicide prevention education for students. Instruction can be embedded in student health curriculum or in safety and wellness classes. As the number of states passing legislation requiring suicide prevention training for school personnel and programs for students increases, implementing the Model Policy will ensure compliance with state laws.

It describes detailed intervention procedures for assessment and referral of at-risk youth. Guidance for handling in-school and out-of-school suicide attempts includes a sequence of steps to follow. It also suggests reentry procedures for students returning to school after a mental health crisis and includes a section on parental notification and involvement.

Postvention procedures for the crisis team to follow if a suicide death occurs prevent possible suicide contagion. Suggestions on how to interact with the family and communicate with the community will help school personnel respond during an emotional time. Schools also need to support students and staff and handle memorial planning appropriately.

The resource section of the Model Policy includes toolkits and guidebooks on prevention, as well as information about relevant research, school programs, crisis services, and working with the media. There's also a sample simplified version of the policy for student handbooks.

ADVOCATING FOR A SCHOOL DISTRICT SUICIDE PREVENTION POLICY

If a district or school has no suicide prevention policy in place, don't assume that someone else will come along and implement one. As an educator, you are in a position to speak for those who can't or won't speak for themselves. Be an advocate. Find out which decision makers in a school or district have the authority to implement a comprehensive policy. Talk to them. Suicide is a difficult topic to discuss, so expect to encounter resistance and don't give up. Be persistent.

Speaking at a school board meeting is a good way to inform the school community about suicide prevention. Prepare for those presentations by assembling talking points and information packets to give to district officials. If you are a school counselor, psychologist, nurse, or teacher, explain your role in suicide prevention. Share youth suicide data. Use it to spell out why suicide prevention in school matters. Offer the Model Policy as a guide the district can use to create a customized policy that will meet the needs of the community.

Follow up by scheduling in-person meetings with key administrators and school board members. Try to make personal connections. Share stories about positive examples of interventions. Engage parents and families—they have a loud voice. Provide data or examples from neighboring schools or districts. Be persistent. Change takes time.

It may not be realistic to expect a district to adopt the entire Model Policy at one time, so it helps to set small incremental goals that are more attainable. Choose an initial area of focus depending on what your district needs most. Start with creation of a suicide prevention task force, funding and/or time off for professional development, increase of school-employed mental health professionals, or increased collaboration among schools and community services.

Advocates may want to go beyond the district level and meet with state legislators. Educate them about the critical need for suicide prevention in schools. Ask for comprehensive legislation that includes training for educators and funding to hire mental health professionals for schools. Again, be persistent.

If you need help in promoting or implementing the Model Policy, just ask. Reach out to the Trevor Project, the American Foundation for Suicide Prevention (AFSP), the American School Counselor Association (ASCA), or the National Association of School Psychologists (NASP).

To find current data and information about state laws on suicide prevention in schools, look at the AFSP website under public policies.[6] Links will take you to state-specific resources. Facts and statistics by state are also available in the About Suicide section.[7]

GETTING STARTED

Once a decision has been reached to adopt a suicide prevention policy, the first step is to assemble a task force led by the district's designated suicide prevention coordinator. Members should represent administrators, parents, teachers, school-employed mental health professionals, representatives from community suicide prevention services, and other experts in youth mental health.

Resources may include prevention policies developed by state education departments, other states, or suicide prevention organizations. Key points from the *Model School District Policy on Suicide Prevention* are described below. Download the most recent edition of the Model Policy for more detailed information.

The primary objective of the task force is to outline a comprehensive suicide prevention policy. The policy will clearly define the way the district addresses suicide prevention. Using the policy as a guide, the team will develop a suicide prevention plan that spells out a course of action and includes details describing how to accomplish each goal.

Once the plan is written and published, inform the school community. Make sure everyone knows the implementation timeline and understands what to expect.

PREVENTION

After the written policy is in place and the district assigns a suicide prevention coordinator to implement it, the focus shifts to increasing awareness throughout the school community. Ideally, all staff will receive annual training on risk factors, warning signs, protective factors, response procedures, referrals, postvention, and resources regarding youth suicide prevention. School-employed mental health professionals and nurses need additional professional development in risk assessment and crisis intervention. Integrate age-appropriate suicide prevention programs for students into the curriculum at all grade levels, K–12. Distribute the policy annually and include it in all student and teacher handbooks and on the school website.

Warning Signs

For adults working with youth, it's difficult to distinguish between typical teenage behavior and actual warning signs. Feelings are often concealed from family members and school staff. Peers are usually the first to notice the warning signs but keep them secret or don't know what action to take. Awareness of typical warning signs is the first step in prevention. Any signs noticed for more than two weeks may signal a serious problem.

- Talking about
    - ◆ Feeling hopeless and wanting to die
    - ◆ Having no reason to live
    - ◆ Being a burden to others
    - ◆ Feeling trapped
    - ◆ Unbearable pain
- Behavior
    - ◆ Increased use of alcohol or drugs
    - ◆ Searching for ways to commit suicide
    - ◆ Withdrawing from normal activities
    - ◆ Isolating from family and friends
    - ◆ Sleeping too much or too little
    - ◆ Visiting or calling people to say good-bye
    - ◆ Giving away prized possessions
    - ◆ Aggression

♦ Fatigue

• Mood

    ♦ Depression
    ♦ Anxiety
    ♦ Loss of interest
    ♦ Irritability
    ♦ Humiliation
    ♦ Agitation
    ♦ Rage

Risk Factors

Risk factors increase the possibility that a person may try to take his or her own life, especially when there are two or more.

• Major depression or bipolar disorder
• Alcohol or drug abuse
• Unusual thoughts and behavior or confusion about reality
• Personality traits that create a pattern of intense, unstable relationships or trouble with the law
• Impulsivity and aggression, especially along with a mental disorder
• Previous suicide attempt or family history of a suicide attempt or mental disorder
• Serious mental condition and/or pain

Note that while certain risk factors are associated with suicide deaths, most people with mental illness or other suicide risk factors are not suicidal.

Protective Factors

Suicide prevention efforts tend to focus on warning signs and risk factors, but protective factors are an essential component in reducing vulnerability to suicidal behavior. Parents, guardians, and educators play an important role in creating an environment where acceptance and caring are an integral part of the school community. Adults who accept and value children regardless of their differences help reinforce that sense of connection. Protective factors may not prevent suicide but can decrease risk.

• Receiving effective mental health care
• Positive connections to family, peers, community, and social institutions
• Resilience
• Problem-solving skills

Awareness and understanding of social and behavioral issues among adolescents helps school-based mental health professionals, administrators, teachers, and staff support students who may be at higher risk. Since mental disorders are often undiagnosed and untreated, school staff trained to identify warning signs and risk factors are better prepared to refer students to treatment.

Mental Disorders

- Depression
- Bipolar
- Alcohol or substance abuse
- Schizophrenia
- Borderline personality disorder
- Conduct disorder
- Anxiety disorder

Youth with Complex Risk Factors

- Self-harm or previous suicide attempts
- Out-of-home settings
    - Juvenile justice
    - Child welfare systems/foster care
    - Homeless/runaway
- American Indian/Alaska Native
    - Substance abuse
    - Discrimination
    - Lack of access to medical care
    - Historical trauma
- LGBTQ
    - Discrimination
    - Family rejection
    - Harassment
    - Bullying
    - Violence
    - Victimization
    - Suicide bereavement
    - Medical conditions or disabilities

Bullying

It has long been assumed that bullying can lead to suicide, but the research points to a much more complex relationship. Both the student who bullies others and the student being bullied may be at risk, but usually only if there are other risk factors involved. Depression, anxiety, substance abuse, and one or more negative life events are likely to be the underlying causes. Most students who are bullied do not become suicidal.

INTERVENTION—ASSESS AND REFER

One way to assess students who might be at risk is to follow up after suicide prevention presentations with middle or high school students. The SOS program[8] includes a simple screening form for use after the presentation. When presenters conduct the screening, schools should plan on having a team of counselors ready. They'll talk with individual students who indicate risk factors or want to talk to a counselor about a friend.

Even if it isn't conducted in conjunction with a presentation, having a system in place to screen all students for risk is an effective strategy. If the school prefers not to do a general screening, then the school mental health professional or nurse might use a screener to assess risk and start the referral process. Staff members trained to identify a student who may be suicidal or respond if the student self-refers should not hesitate to refer them to the school counselor or psychologist.

At-Risk Student

1. School staff will supervise the student to ensure their safety. Never leave the student alone.
2. Notify the principal and suicide prevention coordinator.
3. The school's mental health professional or principal will contact parents and assist them with making a referral for emergency services or mental health care.
4. The school's mental health professional or principal may request a medical release form to discuss the student's health with outside providers, if appropriate.

In-School Suicide Attempts

1. Render first aid and follow district emergency medical procedures.
2. Supervise the student to ensure their safety.
3. Move all other students out of the area.

4. The school's mental health professional or principal will contact parents.
5. Notify the principal and suicide prevention coordinator.
6. Engage the crisis team to assess whether additional steps should be taken.

Out-of-School Suicide Attempts

1. If a staff member finds out about a suicide attempt by a student that is in progress at a location outside of the school, call 911.
2. Inform the student's parent or guardian.
3. Notify the school suicide prevention coordinator and principal.

Parental Notification and Involvement

1. If a student is identified as at risk or has made an attempt, parents or guardians must be informed.
2. The school mental health professional or principal should counsel parents on means restriction—limiting access to weapons, drugs, or other means of self-harm.
3. If the principal or school mental health professional believes that contacting the parent or guardian would endanger the student, they may delay contact.

Reentry after an Attempt

1. The school's mental health professional and principal should meet with parents and the student before they return to a regular class schedule. Together they'll plan reentry and next steps to ensure that support is in place to facilitate the student's transition.
2. Parents will provide documentation from a mental health care provider that the student is no longer in danger.
3. A designated staff person will provide support to the student during the transition back into the school community.

POSTVENTION—AFTER A SUICIDE

When a suicide occurs within the school community, having an action plan in place will help guide the response. The crisis team must meet immediately to develop and implement the plan. Clear and appropriate communication is essential.

Action Plan

- Verify the death

  ♦ Confirmation from the student's parent or guardian, coroner's office, hospital, or police.
  ♦ Ask permission from parents to disclose the death.

- Assess the situation

  ♦ Determine how the death will affect the school and which students are most likely to be affected.
  ♦ Prepare response for the school community.

- Share information

  ♦ The death should be reported to staff without stating the cause until it's confirmed.
  ♦ Prepare a written statement for staff to share with students.
  ♦ Do not use the public address systems or schoolwide assemblies.
  ♦ Prepare a letter to send home, with input from the student's parents, to inform families of the facts. Include information about what the school will do to support students, as well as warning signs of suicidal behavior and resources available in the community.

- Avoid suicide contagion

  ♦ Identify and support high-risk students in the school to prevent another death.

- Initiate support services

  ♦ School mental health professionals should assess at-risk students to determine the support needed.
  ♦ Provide individual or small group counseling.
  ♦ Refer students to community mental health care providers if further support is needed.

- Develop memorial plans

  ♦ To avoid sensationalizing the death and discourage contagion, the school should not create on-campus physical memorials or cancel school for the funeral.
  ♦ School-based memorials should focus on how to prevent future suicides and provide resources.

Communication Plan

- A designated spokesperson will be responsible for all media communication.

    - ◆ Keep the district suicide prevention coordinator and superintendent informed.
    - ◆ Prepare a statement for the media that includes facts of the death, postvention plans, and resources available. Do not disclose personal information or details about the suicide.
    - ◆ Answer all media inquiries.
    - ◆ Encourage reporters not to emphasize the suicide, speculate about the reason, or sensationalize it.
    - ◆ Ask reporters to include information on risk factors, warning signs, and resources in their reporting.

LET THE STUDENTS IN ON THE PLAN

The school's student handbook should include information about the suicide prevention policy. Because students are more likely to search online to find information, the best place to post the suicide prevention portion of the student handbook is on the school's website. For an excellent example, visit Virginia's Fairfax County Public Schools website.[9] The Model Policy provides content that schools can adapt to fit into existing handbooks. Serving as a resource for students, it should reference the main points of the policy.

- Students will learn about recognizing and responding to warning signs of suicide in friends, using coping skills, using support systems, and seeking help for themselves and friends.
- Each school will have a suicide prevention coordinator.
- When a student is identified as being at risk, a school-employed mental health professional will assess the student and help them connect to appropriate local resources.
- Students will have access to national resources they can contact for support, such as:

    - ◆ The National Suicide Prevention Lifeline—1-800-273-TALK (8255)
    - ◆ The Trevor Lifeline—1-866-488-7386
    - ◆ Crisis Text Line—741741

- When students participate in creating a school culture of respect and support, they are comfortable seeking help for themselves or friends. Schools will encourage their students to tell any staff member if they, or a friend, are feeling suicidal or in need of help.

• Students should also know that because of the life-or-death nature of these matters, seeking help is more important than confidentiality or privacy concerns.

AVOID SUICIDE CONTAGION OR "COPYCAT SUICIDES"

Media coverage can trigger contagion if stories about suicide deaths are sensationalized, highly detailed, and repeated often. However, if the school district spokesperson offers reporters guidelines for how to report on suicides responsibly, the risk is substantially diminished. A more positive approach is for media reports to treat the death as a public health issue, include a list of warning signs, and encourage self-help. They may also provide hotline phone and texting numbers. Saying the person "died by suicide" is preferable to the term "committed suicide." Refer reporters to Reporting on Suicide.org,[10] a website providing further recommendations on how to report on suicide.

Schools can reduce the risk of contagion by focusing on the connection between mental health issues like depression and anxiety rather than memorializing the death. All deaths—whether accidental or the result of a disease—should be treated the same way, regardless of the cause. The spokesperson may refer to the American Foundation for Suicide Prevention's *After a Suicide* resource guide for sample notification statements.[11]

Encourage parents and guardians to monitor their child's social networking pages. Students are likely to express their thoughts and feelings to others on social media. Ask parents and students to report any warning signs of suicidal behavior to the school. The suicide prevention coordinator will consult with the crisis team about supporting other students who may be at risk.

STATE LAWS AND THEIR EFFECT ON RISK FACTORS

Referral to mental health care providers is a critical component in suicide prevention. In many states, however, access to care may be limited. Youth under eighteen must have parental permission to receive mental health care and confidentiality is not protected. LGBTQ youth lacking parental support may struggle to find the care they need. So although the number of states requiring suicide prevention training for school personnel is increasing, it is important to be aware of challenges that may occur while seeking professional health care for students.

In addition, in some states antidiscrimination laws in conjunction with antibullying and harassment laws prohibit educators from discussing LGBTQ issues in stigmatizing ways. In states lacking such laws, LGBTQ youth are less likely to seek help from teachers and school staff.

Schools have been sued for negligence and found liable in several court cases. Negligence for not warning parents or failing to provide supervision and counseling for suicidal students have been the most common causes. Failure to reduce bullying and harassment have also led to legal action.

BARRIERS TO SUICIDE PREVENTION IN SCHOOLS

To develop and implement any new comprehensive plan is a second order change in a school. Resistance to change is normal and expected, regardless of the reason for doing it. Because suicide is such a sensitive topic, pushback stems from specific reasons. School leaders seeking to initiate a suicide prevention plan will be better prepared to respond if they know what the reactions are likely to be.

Awareness

If you still think suicide is one of those things that happen to other people, far outside your immediate circle, think again. Just do the math. If the most recent figure, 44,000 deaths, were divided equally among fifty states—each one would have close to a thousand each year. Of course, the number includes all suicide deaths, not just youth, but any suicide death in a community will touch the school in some way. How many school districts are there in your state? What if one or two of those deaths happened in yours, how would you feel? What would you do about it? Not being prepared for a crisis means that we are reactive instead of proactive and not thinking clearly in the immediacy of an unexpected event.

Time

Finding time to add another class or special presentation is a constant challenge for every school. While it seems logical to add suicide prevention lessons to a mental health module, all schools don't follow a health curriculum or offer health classes. Because of the pressure to demonstrate learning through high-stakes testing in reading and math, other subjects are relegated to the back burner. Teachers have to figure out how to cover all of the required content in the time allocated for their subject areas. Adding mental health lessons often means leaving out something else.

Money

School districts are constantly under pressure to do more with less. After the crash of 2008, budgets in many states got slashed to a fraction of what they once were. If districts had counselors or social workers, those positions were the first to be cut. While the economy in most parts of the country has recovered, school funding has not. Budget increases have yet to replace the lost funding. Hiring mental health professionals for every school in a district means exchanging the salary of a teacher for a counselor. Fewer teachers leads to larger class sizes, and districts are understandably reluctant to make that exchange.

Stigma

The stigma of suicide remains a silent constraint for many communities. People fear that if they talk about suicide out loud, it will happen. The cultural beliefs are so strong that even with the increasing awareness about mental illness in our society, many still consider suicide an act of cowardice. School leaders are reluctant to bring up a subject that will cause a negative reaction. Despite their knowledge about the importance of prevention, they prefer to let sleeping dogs lie.

Administrators who acknowledge and address each barrier are more likely to gain cooperation from school staff. Overcoming them will lead to a safer and more positive environment for students.

Please see chapter 10 on resources for a comprehensive list of materials available to schools.

Suicide Can Be Prevented.
Know the Warning Signs, Risk Factors, and Protective Factors.

If you are suicidal or you think someone you know is, help is available, and recovery is possible.
Learn the warning signs, and do whatever you can to get yourself or someone you care about the help they need so that they can return to living a fully functioning life.

EMERGENCY 911 — **Call 9-1-1 or seek immediate help from a mental health provider if you or someone you know:**

Threatens to hurt or kill him/herself, or talks about wanting to hurt or kill him/herself

Looks for ways to kill him/herself by seeking access to firearms, available pills, or other means

Talks or writes about death, dying, or suicide

Figure 4.1. Suicide Can Be Prevented

WARNING SIGNS

Seek help by contacting a mental health professional or calling 1-800-273-TALK (8255) if you notice any one or more of these behaviors in yourself or someone you care about:

- Hopelessness
- Rage, uncontrolled anger
- Reckless or risky activities, seemingly without thinking
- Feeling trapped - like there's no way out
- Increased alcohol or drug use
- Withdrawal from friends, family, and society
- Anxiety, agitation, unable to sleep or sleeping all the time
- Dramatic mood changes
- Feeling unimportant or overwhelmed
- Giving away most valuable possessions
- Losing interest in favorite things to do
- Admiring people who have died by suicide
- Planning for death by writing a will or letter

Not caring about the future: "It won't matter soon anyway."

Put-downs: "I don't deserve to live. I suck."

Hopelessness: "Things will never get better for me."

Saying goodbye: "You're the best friend I've ever had. I'll miss you."

Having a specific plan for suicide: "I've thought about how I'd do it."

Talking about feeling suicidal: "Life is so hard. Lately, I've felt like ending it all."

RISK FACTORS

Risk factors increase the chances that you or someone you know could die by suicide.

- Mental disorders; particularly mood disorders, depression, bipolar, schizophrenia, anxiety disorders, and certain personality disorders
- Alcohol and other substance use disorder
- Local clusters of suicide
- Lack of social support and sense of isolation
- Stigma associated with asking for help
- Lack of health care, especially mental health and substance abuse treatment
- Cultural and religious beliefs, such as the belief that suicide is a noble resolution of a personal dilemma
- Exposure to others who have died by suicide (in real life or via the media and Internet)
- Impulsive and/or aggressive tendencies
- History of trauma or abuse
- Major physical illnesses or chronic illnesses
- Previous suicide attempt
- Family history of suicide
- Recent job or financial loss
- Recent loss of relationship
- Easy access to lethal means
- Non-suicidal self-injury
- Homelessness
- High-stress family environment
- Academic or family crisis
- Victimization at home or in school
- Difficulty in school, failing grades, bullying others
- Unwillingness to seek help

PROTECTIVE FACTORS

Protective factors make you or someone you know less likely to engage in suicidal behavior. They can promote resilience and make you feel connected with others during difficult times.

- Effective clinical care for mental, physical and substance use disorders
- Easy access to a variety of clinical interventions
- Support through ongoing medical and mental health care relationships
- Restricted access to highly lethal means of suicide
- Strong connections to family and community support
- Skills in coping, problem-solving, conflict resolution and handling problems in a non-violent way
- Cultural and religious beliefs that discourage suicide and support self-preservation
- Connectedness to safe schools
- A feeling of safety, support and connectivity at school through peer groups
- Positive connections with friends who share similar interests
- Academic, artistic, athletic achievements
- Family acceptance for sexual orientation and/or gender identity
- Cultural and religious beliefs that discourage suicide
- Positive role models
- Strong self-esteem

The School Counselor and Suicide Prevention/Awareness
(Adopted 2018)

American School Counselor Association (ASCA) Position
School counselors work to identify behavioral and social/emotional signs of suicide risk among their students and ensure prevention methods are in place. It is the school counselor's ethical and moral responsibility to report suspected suicide risk to legal guardians and the appropriate authorities. In acknowledging suspected suicide risk, school counselors exercise reasonable care to protect students from unforeseeable harm (ASCA, 2016).

The Rationale
According to the Centers for Disease Control (CDC, 2015), suicide is the second leading cause of death for young peo-ple between the ages of 15 and 35 and the second leading cause of death for youth ages 10 to 14. Overall the nation has seen a 24 percent increase in suicide completions over the past 15 years (CDC, 2015). Data from the 2015 National Youth Risk Behavior Surveillance Survey (YRBSS) showed that 29.9 percent or three out of 10 U.S. high school students expressed feeling sad or hopeless almost daily for two or more weeks (CDC, 2015). In addition, CDC (2015) reported that 17.7 percent of students expressed suicide ideation, and 14.6 percent of students had completed plans for their suicide. These statistics are alarming and reveal that students in significant numbers experience feelings and thoughts that isolate and lead to suicidal ideation and plans. Raising awareness around suicide and implementing suicide prevention initiatives is important in reinforcing student support and safety measures.

The School Counselor's Role
School counselors recognize the threat of suicide among children and adolescents and strive to create a supportive environment. School counselors do not wait for certainty but rather the notion of a potential suicide places school counselors in a position to immediately notify parents/guardians (ASCA 2017). School counselors contact parents/guardians when placed on notice that a suicide is possible through student self-report, peer report, rumors, hearsay or any other means. It is a well-known fact that students will often deny suicidal ideation to escape the gaze of adults while confiding their true intentions to their peers. School counselors provide parents/guardians with referral resources for students (Stone, 2018). In the case that the parents/guardians do not take seriously the potential threat, the school counselor makes a report to child protective service (Stone, 2018). School counselors work to raise awareness of suicide and suicide ideation, train school personnel and create opportunities to identify resources available for school personnel (Desrochers & Houck, 2013).

To achieve their ethical obligation to protect students, school counselors must maintain current training in:
- Being informed about signs of suicidal thoughts
- Being knowledgeable about the resources available
- Preparing students, staff, colleagues and parents to recognize warning symptoms for suicidal behavior
- Referring students who demonstrate signs of suicidal thoughts to local community agencies

Summary
Through the implementation of comprehensive suicide prevention/awareness, school counselors ensure students and faculty are well-prepared to address and identify the negative thoughts and experiences that could potentially lead a student to suicide ideation.

References
American School Counselor Association. (2016). *Ethical standards for school counselors.* Retrieved from
https://www.schoolcounselor.org/asca/media/asca/Ethics/EthicalStandards2016.pdf

American School Counselor Association. (2017). Retrieved from
http://webcache.googleusercontent.com/search?q=cache:h0kMsfUXhJIJ:schoolcounselor.org/asca/media/asca/Resource e%2520Center/Suicide-Suicide%2520Prevention/Sample%2520Documents/FAQs.doc+&cd=2&hl=en&ct=clnk&gl=us

Figure 4.2. From the School Counselor and Suicide Prevention/Awareness position statement (Adopted 2018) American School Counselor Association

Centers for Disease Control and Prevention. (2015). Youth risk behavior surveillance system data: Adolescent and school health. Retrieved from https://www.cdc.gov/healthyyouth/data/yrbs/index.htm

Desrochers J., & Houck G. (2013). Depression in children and adolescents: Guidelines for school practice: Principal leadership. Retrieved from http://www.nasponline.org/resources/principals/April_13_Depression.pdf

Population Reference Bureau. (2016). Suicide replaces homicide as second-leading cause of death among U.S. teenagers. Retrieved from http://www.prb.org/Publications/Articles/2016/suicide-replaces-homicide-second-leading-cause-death-among-us-teens.aspx

Stone, C. (2018). *Assessments and Third Party Software Alerts for Suicide Ideation.* ASCA January/February 2018.

Resources

"13 Reasons Why" and the Role of the School Counselor to Combat Teen Suicide. (2017, July 2). Retrieved February 27, 2018, from https://counseling.online.wfu.edu/blog/13-reasons-why-and-the-role-of-the-school-counselor-to-combat-teen-suicide/

Chapter Five

Intervention

HOW TO HELP A SUICIDAL STUDENT

Possibly the hardest part of suicide prevention for schools is intervening when a student is at risk. While warning signs and risk factors help identify a student who is struggling, the reasons for suicidal thoughts are different for every person. Intervention means taking action and getting involved.

If you notice a student whose behavior is not typical, mention your concerns. Tell them you are concerned about them. Ask the student if they've thought about harming themselves. Depending on the response, sometimes it's enough to sit and listen. If you believe there may be a risk, never leave a student alone, even to step away to get help. Contact another staff member and request assistance from the school's mental health professional, nurse, or administrator.

The school's mental health professional will perform a formal suicide risk assessment (SRA).[1] Contact parents to inform them of the risk level and recommend a referral to community mental health providers.

EXPERT COMMENTARY: KELLY VAILLANCOURT STROHBACH, DIRECTOR OF POLICY AND ADVOCACY, NATIONAL ASSOCIATION OF SCHOOL PSYCHOLOGISTS (NASP)

After starting out as a school psychologist, Kelly felt strongly that school psychologists should not be limited to acting as gatekeepers for special education. They should be empowered to provide a broader range of services to all students. Her passion led to her current position with the National Association of School Psychologists where she leads advocacy efforts and promotes policy goals that advance the role of school psychologists. [2] NASP seeks to increase access to comprehensive school psychological services that improve academic, behavioral, social-emotional, and mental health outcomes of children and youth.

Schools Need Access to Mental Health Services

"Prevention is cheaper than intervention in a lot of ways."

Having access to mental health professionals will save a school district money in the long run. When schools don't have access to these professionals on an adequate level, students are not getting the help and services they need until they're in crisis. At that point, it's too late to pull them back without intensive mental and behavioral health support.

But if you have folks on the frontline who can help early on, it makes a difference. Teachers are the first line of defense. They spend almost as much time with children during the week as their parents do, and sometimes they're the first ones to notice something is a little bit concerning. Their referrals to mental health professionals at school can make the difference between prevention and intervention.

Teachers can ask for help if they know there's a school psychologist, or a counselor, or social worker they should go to the second they're worried about a student. That person can come in, consult with the family and the teacher, and speak with the child. They can very quickly say, "You know what, this is just a situational thing. They're having a hard time at home, or they had a bad day with a friend." Or they can say, "This was a red flag, thank you for catching it." They're in a position to put plans in place to support the student right away.

For the longest time, having access to mental and behavioral health support and focusing on social-emotional learning was viewed as a luxury, an add-on, something that wasn't necessary for schools. Today administrators really need to rethink that. Not only do schools have to teach kids the skills they need to get a job, but they also have to teach them the skills they need to keep a job. From that perspective, social-emotional learning and mental and behavioral health are as important as academics.

If a district doesn't have access to mental health services on each campus, they may want to take a look at the budget. They could reprioritize what they're spending money on to make sure every school has access to school-employed mental health professionals. Not that one type of curriculum is more important than the other and without discounting the importance of foreign language curriculum or a wide variety of athletics. But it is worth considering. Research shows that school counselors, school psychologists, and school social workers are often the first positions to go when schools face budget cuts. That's a really shortsighted decision.

Clearly, having access to school-employed mental health professionals is absolutely critical. But in many of our communities, there is a shortage of mental health professionals. Not just in terms of school psychologists, social workers, and counselors but also child and adolescent psychiatrists and other community-based mental health professionals. It's unrealistic to think they'll hire a counselor, psychologist, and a social worker for every school. So in those communities, districts need to get creative.

If a school can't sustain full-time staff members, they can forge partnerships with community-based resources to bring help into the school. Even one day a week will help. Doing something to make sure students are getting seen early makes more sense than waiting until they're having a mental health crisis, or they've made a suicide threat. With the right people in place, signs are caught early.

The long-term goal would be for schools and districts to make it a priority to employ school psychologists/counselors/social workers full-time. School community partnerships should not be a substitute for full-time mental health professionals in schools, but they can certainly help fill a need.

There's been an emergence of telehealth and telepsychology services, which can connect kids to professionals through FaceTime or Google Hangouts on their phones or computers. There are a lot of HIPAA (Health Insurance Portability and Accountability) compliant apps to make sure therapists are abiding by the right privacy laws and safeguarding sensitive information. The technology is available, but because it is so new, there's not much research on it yet. In communities where one school district might be five hundred square miles, and there is one school and one professional serving all the students, it could be a viable option for them.

The Real Role of a School Psychologist

> "When people think of a school psychologist, they think special education, assessment for special education, and working primarily with kids in special education. That's certainly part of their role, but it's not all they do."

When the ratio is very high, over 1 to 4,500, school psychologists are just doing special education assessment and dealing with kids in crisis. In places where the ratio is closer to the recommended ratio of 1 school psychologist for every 500 to 700 students, school psychologists can provide a much broader range of services.

School psychologists are integral members of the school team. They are skilled in providing direct services to students, as well as indirect services via consultation with teachers, administrators, parents and families, and other school staff to help meet the academic, social, emotional, mental, and behavioral health needs of students.

This often includes being part of school-level or district-level teams looking at school safety and climate issues. School psychologists support suicide prevention and threat assessment by providing professional development to teachers and staff, as well as working directly with students.

As site-based professionals, school psychologists, sometimes along with school counselors, will go into classrooms and provide psychological education on a variety of topics. They teach students how to recognize signs and risk factors of suicidal thoughts, the differences between typical versus troubled behavior, and how to refer themselves or others for help. This is especially true for middle and high school students because they spend more time with their friends than anybody else. They need to know some of the red flags to look for in their friends and when to tell an adult. Framing it as "you're not snitching, you're not going to get in trouble, you're not telling on somebody; what you're really doing is helping your friend" encourages students to take action.

Behavioral consultations and providing assistance with intervention development are important parts of a school psychologist's job. They're often members of child study teams working with educators to design high-quality, evidence-based intervention plans for struggling students. They may not always be the one actually delivering the intervention—it might be the teacher, it might be the school counselor, or it might be somebody else. Psychologists can also help monitor the implementation, track student progress, and make adjustments when needed.

School psychologists do individual and group counseling with children and adolescents for a variety of issues. They range from basic study skills, anger management, and social skills, all the way up to kids struggling with anxiety disorders or depression. Sometimes this is done in collaboration with the school counselor and the school social worker, especially if it's group counseling.

School psychologists are involved with crisis preparedness and crisis intervention too. They provide support when there is any kind of large-scale crisis in the school, from something as awful as a school shooting to wildfires, floods, or other disasters. The psychologists provide direct crisis intervention services to students ranging from triage to long-term follow-up after a crisis. They work with administrators to make sure they're ready when the students come back to school. Together they plan for the support they'll need to have in place for students and staff.

At the heart of it, school psychologists work with parents, families, teachers, administrators, and other school staff to implement and deliver supports students need in order to learn and be successful. There's some overlap in what school counselors and school psychologists do, but they play very distinct roles. The biggest difference is that psychologists tend to provide more intensive mental and behavioral health services, whereas school counselors are often the tier one supports on the prevention, early intervention side.

If a situation gets more severe, the school psychologist has the training to handle it. Sometimes that involves making referrals and collaborating or communicating with providers in the community. Counselors tend to focus more on academic counseling, career counseling, and college readiness—all of the details that deal with a student's career trajectory. In a perfect world, every school would have one of each.

Viable Options for Schools with Limited Resources

> "Students might need short-term help at some point throughout the school year. It's unfair and harmful to make them wait until they hit crisis mode before you get them help."

In some districts where resources are severely limited, school psychologists and counselors maintain such high caseloads that they simply can't do more than testing or academic counseling. It is unrealistic to expect them to focus on social-emotional learning or mental and behavioral health. They must look for resources available in their communities.

There are organizations that can help, like Communities in Schools[3] and the Coalition for Community Schools.[4] They recommend conducting a comprehensive needs assessment. Start by looking at what resources a school already has and what services they are already providing for their students. Then compare that to the needs of the school and the community.

The next step is to go out into the community and try to identify agencies who could supplement what isn't available in the school. Schools can partner with a nonprofit or the local mental health agency by developing a cooperative agreement that allows them to provide services at the direction of the school district.

Some partnerships may only involve tier three students, those in need of the most intensive mental and behavioral health support. That may free up time for the counselor and psychologist to do more intervention and prevention work. Sometimes it's the only mental health services the school can provide, but that's when schools need to get creative.

It is a mistake for schools or districts to think all they need is a community partnership to focus on their students in crisis. That's a shortsighted decision. While those kids in crisis absolutely need support and care, the other 80 percent of the students in the school might need short-term help at some point throughout the school year. It's unfair and harmful to those students to make them wait until they hit crisis mode before you get them help. Even when resources are limited, districts should focus on the long-term goal of seeking funding to employ as many full-time, school-employed mental health professionals as they can.

In situations where a district has not yet developed partnerships with other agencies, has no mental health professionals on staff other than a school nurse, and a teacher identifies a student with risk factors for suicidal behavior, someone has to intervene. Administrators or school nurses can start to connect kids with support while they're working with whomever is available to find a mental health professional. Ethically, educators should not do anything beyond what they are trained to do.

If there isn't a mental health professional available, any staff member can be a good mentor to the student, a good listener, and a trusted adult. While they should not be attempting to engage in therapy with them, at a minimum they can try to forge a relationship. The student might be more comfortable coming to them when they are worried about themselves or someone else. In that kind of situation, the student knows there is someone they can talk to until resources in the community can be found.

What administrators should never do is say they can't help and shut the student down. It's important to foster a good relationship and show they're doing everything they can to find the help the student needs. Hopefully, administrators would take advantage of the various mental health hotlines out there and pass those on to the student. The national hotlines have trained counselors or trained listeners answering the phone. They are certainly better than having no one for the student to talk to until they can be connected with a mental healthcare provider in the community.

Advocate for Mental Health Professionals

> "We have got to be teaching kids appropriate conflict resolution and how to effectively manage their emotions so they can go on to be functioning and emotionally healthy young people."

At the federal level, NASP has been encouraging the Department of Education and the Department of Health and Human Services, the Substance Abuse and Mental Health Services Administration (SAMHSA), and Congress to allocate increased funding for mental health. Grants can be used to train mental and behavioral health professionals to increase the workforce, as well as provide various investments to local school districts. Schools should be allowed to hire mental and behavioral health professionals with that money if it's something they need.

Most of the action in this space has happened at the state level. Since many personnel and hiring decisions are made at the state level, NASP helps the state associations articulate to state-level lawmakers the value of having access to mental health professionals. They encourage developing or having their states change the funding formulas to allow for more professionals to be hired and to create training grants.

A lot of states have been successful in implementing things like mental health first aid and improved suicide prevention training. Not all have achieved the ratio of 1 school psychologist for every 500 to 700 students, but many districts around the country follow NASP recommendations. They build a great team of counselors, psychologists, and social workers who all work together to meet the comprehensive mental and behavioral health needs of students. Sharing those stories will help district leaders learn from each other. The value of making the investment in mental health professionals at their schools is obvious.

Recent school shootings have heightened concern around the importance of school mental health. It's important to separate the conversation around school safety and school mental health to avoid a perpetuated stigma that kids with mental health issues are violent. That's not true. Schools need to teach students appropriate conflict resolution and how to effectively manage their emotions. Teachers need to learn how to recognize signs, so the small percentage of students that do exhibit violent tendencies benefit from interventions early. With the right support, they can be moved off the pathway to violence and go on to be functioning and emotionally healthy young people.

Ongoing Professional Learning

Although school psychologists and counselors receive training in crisis intervention and suicide prevention as part of their graduate education, it's kind of like learning a foreign language. You can graduate from college fluent in Spanish but if you don't use your Spanish you start to lose it, and your skills get a little rusty.

So while school counselors and school psychologists are well trained and well equipped to meet the needs of students in crisis, it's important that they get ongoing professional development. Just as administrators want teachers to stay on top of evidence-based curriculum and reading instruction strategies, they also need to make sure school psychologists and counselors know about evidenced-based suicide risk, suicide risk assessment, threat assessment, and the newest counseling techniques. It's important that they stay on the cutting edge of research and make sure that whatever interventions they use with students are grounded in research.

Boston Public Schools Comprehensive Behavioral Health Model

"The Boston Public Schools Comprehensive Behavioral Health Model is the gold star, the platinum star!"[5]

The Boston Public Schools (BPS) Comprehensive Behavioral Health Model is the gold standard. It's probably taken them fifteen or twenty years to get to where they are, but they have a school psychologist at almost every school now. Each demonstrates the comprehensive role of the school psychologist by expanding the broad range of knowledge and skills they can provide.[6]

It's a comprehensive system of support that includes the school counselor, the school psychologist, and community partners. They have an incredible network of community partners. Although they're not employed by the district, they are seen as vital members of the school community.

BPS has a seamless system of care. When there is a student approaching crisis who needs tier three services, there's somebody already there to provide those services. They also maintain a great relationship with Boston Children's Hospital, so if a situation rises to that level, they connect kids with support quickly. BPS has incredible data on the positive outcomes of the Comprehensive Behavioral Health Model (CBHM). It all stemmed from the amount of trauma they were seeing in their youth as the result of community violence almost two decades ago.

When a district is thinking about how they can improve their comprehensive mental and behavioral health work, NASP is quick to recommend looking at the Boston Public Schools Comprehensive Behavioral Health Model. They are unique in that they're in an urban setting and have access to universities, a hospital, as well as a number of community agencies. Not every community has that, but they can look at Boston for ideas on how they set up the model, how they utilized existing resources, and how they went into the community to supplement support.

Turn a Vision into Reality

"This work can take time. Stick with it."

A positive relationship with the school board and the superintendent is critical to success. Integration of social-emotional learning and building effective teams to support mental and behavioral health doesn't happen quickly and results may not be easily measured initially. Decision makers at the district level need to understand that it will take several years to see noticeable changes. The payoff, in the long run, is providing a strong infrastructure that translates into better academic achievement and overall growth for students.

Administrators at all levels need to keep the conversation going. They must constantly remind their school boards why social-emotional learning and mental and behavioral health is important and how having mental health professionals in schools will help students succeed. It's not enough just to believe in it. It takes continuous effort and action to turn a vision into reality.

PARENTS HAVE THE RIGHT TO KNOW

There are times educators must decide whether to inform parents that their child is struggling emotionally, fearing the source of the problems may be the home life. However, unless there is evidence that informing parents would cause further harm, schools are legally obligated to do so. A risk assessment will indicate if a student is at no risk, low, moderate, or high risk and guide the decisions about next steps. Regardless of the results of the assessment, parents must be informed it has been conducted.

Relationships between parents and teachers are built on trust. Parents want to believe the school is taking care of their child and appreciate being informed of any concerns. If parents sometimes believe the student's behavior is simply attention seeking and see no need for taking action, they are likely to think they can resolve the issue on their own. Teachers and administrators need to understand parents are trying to do what's best even if they don't agree with their choices.

It is important to encourage parents to seek treatment regardless of the age or past behavior of the child. School administrators are justifiably wary of making any kind of medical recommendations, but they can expect parents to follow up with a medical or behavioral health assessment and care plan. After an intervention, schools often request documentation that a student has been evaluated by a mental health professional before returning to school.

INTERVENTION PLANS BASED ON RISK ASSESSMENT RESULTS

No Risk

Although it is not uncommon to hear a student say "I wish I were dead," that statement may reflect a recent frustration or disappointment rather than real suicidal ideation. Likewise, just because a student suffers from anxiety and depression, it does not mean they are likely to die by suicide.

Even students who intentionally cut or burn themselves, or self-harm in other ways, are not necessarily at risk of suicide. A risk assessment can alleviate concern or identify a level of risk that will guide the next steps a school should take.

Low Risk

A student considered to be at low risk may have occasional suicidal thoughts but has not considered a plan. The school should work with the student and parents to create a safety plan. Equally important is to provide a list of community resources and encourage parents to seek mental health care for the student.

If care is already in place, they should inform their provider of the incident. Just as with any serious health issue, it's advisable to request a signed medical information release form. By allowing the health care provider to share treatment information with the school, staff can better monitor the student and take appropriate action while the student is on campus.

Moderate Risk

If the results of the risk assessment show a student is at moderate risk, he has had frequent thoughts of suicide. He may be considering plans but has not yet taken action to put them in place. If prompted, he may be able to list positive aspects of his life and identify protective factors available.

The initial intervention steps follow the same guidelines as for a lower risk student, including creating a safety plan and helping parents access community resources to find mental health care. Medication and family therapy may be options at this level. Both the student and his family or guardians should have access to 24-hour crisis services either through a local hospital or phone hotline.

In addition, school mental health professionals or other trusted adults should increase visits with the student. During each meeting, it's important to reevaluate risk level and determine if the child has moved into a lower or higher risk category. Regular communication with parents and community health providers will help keep all adults involved in the student's care informed and aware of any changes.

High Risk

When a student has frequent and enduring thoughts of suicide, a specific plan with access to the means to carry it out, and can't identify any protective factors, they require immediate intervention. School staff must supervise the student at all times while on campus. Contact parents and make arrangements to transport the student to a hospital or mental health facility for evaluation.

It is likely that in time of crisis parents will react with shock or denial, thinking they will be blamed for failing to recognize their child's distress. Or they may show frustration if this isn't the first attempt. Positive interaction with parents during a crisis will help build a foundation of trust for the future. School administrators may feel a sense of urgency and want to insist the parents take action to get help for their child right away. Take a breath, give parents time to process the news, and validate their responses. Whether they felt blindsided by the situation or deny there is cause for real concern, listen and be supportive.

If parents are not willing to transport the student or allow school personnel to make arrangements, it may be necessary to request transportation from child protective services or law enforcement.

Protective Factors

Protective factors provide support. Schools that intentionally focus on strengthening those factors find more opportunities to intervene with suicidal teens. Look for ways to help students make connections with others. Teach real problem-solving skills. Build partnerships with mental health care providers in the community.

Connectedness

Individuals feel valued in a positive school environment. Built on acceptance and caring, it provides the foundation for social relationships. It's those connections within the school community that give young people a sense of belonging and self-worth. Along with caring teachers and staff, interest groups and clubs led by adults or students play an important role too. Kids engaged in activities with others want to fit in and appreciate being part of a group.

Be aware of loners who avoid participating in group activities. Seek out those students and help them connect with others sharing similar interests. Create new groups or projects to get them involved. If teens suffering from a sense of worthlessness make just one connection, it gives them a lifeline to grab on to.

Life Skills and Resilience

Beyond academics, students need to learn basic health and wellness skills like nutrition and exercise. They also need social skills. Coping in social situations and conflict resolution are not innate. Resilience to adapt to stress and adversity can be taught. While a positive self-image and optimism are harder traits to teach, the effort will be worth it.

Effective Mental Health Care

Access to mental health care is not only a protective factor, but it's critical for students in crisis. Schools can help families identify the right community providers. It helps if they tap into the established relationships already in place. The counselor or school nurse should follow up to be sure students are receiving the care they need.

PEER-BASED INTERVENTION

Since teens are more likely to talk to each other than go to an adult if they are struggling, peer-based intervention models are effective in helping students build protective influences. Adult advisors support students participating in the group, oversee messaging and activities, and recruit student leaders.

It's important to include teens from all social groups, not just the high achievers most likely to volunteer. Engage participants representing all grades, racial and ethnic groups, gender identities, and sexual orientations. Also, seek out students who may be less connected to school along with the popular kids.

Training for youth leaders is the core of peer-based intervention. They need to learn how to talk with peers about solving problems and help-seeking behavior. The goal is to eliminate suicide as a solution to seemingly insurmountable problems.

Commercial programs are available but school counselors or teacher leaders could develop their own models. The program can stand alone or be a part of a comprehensive peer mentoring program. Once a school has implemented peer-based intervention, integrating it into the school culture will sustain it over time.

GROUPS AT HIGHER RISK

Many young people suffer from stress caused by prejudice, discrimination, bullying, and violence, either by family members, peers, or the community. The risk increases if they are lesbian, gay, bisexual, or transgender. Suicide rates among Native Americans are among the highest of any ethnic group, especially in the fifteen to twenty-four age group. These students benefit from additional efforts by the school staff to develop and strengthen protective factors.

CREATING A SAFETY PLAN

What Not to Do

Some schools follow a policy that students who report suicidal ideation or harm themselves must be suspended out of school, fearing they may harm others if they remain on campus. Such policies are outdated and based on a negative discipline model. In a culture of caring, school personnel recognize that suspending a student at risk of self-harm only amplifies their issues. If students think they will be punished for sharing their feelings, it is unlikely they will let adults know they are struggling or suffering from a mental illness. If parents take the student out of school to seek treatment and allow time for the student to recover, that's different and may result in more positive outcomes.

What to Do

A safety plan is most effective when created by the student with input and guidance from school mental health professionals. The counselor will ask questions about the triggers, thoughts, feelings, and behaviors the student experienced during the suicidal crisis. Responses are listed along with coping strategies that helped in the past, both internal and from trusted people the student is close to. A list of protective factors includes activities the youth sees as positive that will distract them from suicidal thoughts. Names of people they feel safe confiding in are also written down.

Another part of the plan is an agreement to remove lethal means from the home. If the coping strategies fail to bring relief from suicidal thoughts, emergency numbers to call must be clearly visible. The list should include a parent, close friend, the National Suicide Prevention Lifeline 1-800-273-TALK (8255), and the Crisis Text Line 741741. The safety plan also includes the name and contact information for the nearest emergency room or mental health care facility.

By signing the plan, the student agrees to follow the safety plan when experiencing suicidal thoughts. The parent, school mental health professional, and school administrator provide support and keep monitoring the student as long as necessary.

RESISTANCE

Sometimes, no matter how hard we try, some youth flatly refuse to seek help from a counselor or psychiatrist. Asking for help makes them think they'll become a burden to others. Or they fear people will label them as crazy.

There are others who are receiving treatment but may not be entirely open with their provider or family members. They pretend to be doing well when in reality they are severely depressed. You may know of parents and family members who did everything they possibly could to help their child, but in the end, the illness was too strong to overcome. We have learned from survivors of suicide attempts that they were convinced death was the only way to end their suffering.

When that happens, we grieve deeply for the loss and wonder what more we could have done. There are no easy answers to that question. We can learn from the experience and keep on trying, hoping we will save the next one.

AUTHOR'S NOTE: I WISH I HAD KNOWN THEN WHAT I KNOW NOW

So many times I've wished I had known then what I know now. As a young parent, I was incredibly unaware of mental illness and did not know children could suffer from diagnosable anxiety or depression. It never occurred to me that the first time my ten-year-old son said he wanted to die, I should have seen it as a real concern and taken him to a good therapist. I was worried, of course, and I didn't totally ignore his comment. I asked the school counselor if he would talk to him and give me some advice.

The counselor worked part-time at the school and never did find the time to talk to my son. He gave me a little pink laminated card with emergency information the school district provided. I should have had the sense to take him to a therapist then. I didn't. I don't remember him talking about wanting to die again, and I assumed his suicidal thoughts must have passed. I was wrong.

Those feelings were always there, but my quiet boy just kept them to himself. I know now that he suffered from anxiety all through childhood, although I'm not sure when the depression first set in. My advice to parents and school personnel: please take any mention of suicide seriously. Statistics prove that children as young as eight may have suicidal ideation. Believe it or not, suicide is the second leading cause of death for children ages ten to fourteen.

Individual Student Safety Plan

Name: _____ **Date:** _____

🧠 TRIGGERS
1. Think of the most recent suicidal crisis. Write a short description of what triggered the crisis.

🧠 SUICIDAL THOUGHTS, BEHAVIORS
2. What are the thoughts, emotions, or behaviors that let you (and those around you) know you were in crisis?

Figure 5.1. Individual Safety Plan Form. *Source:* Adapted by permission from Taylor and Francis Group LLC Books, *Suicide in Schools: A Practitioner's Guide to Multi-level Prevention, Assessment, Intervention, and Postvention*, by Terri A. Erbacher, Jonathan B. Singer, and Scott Poland, 2015, 220–21.

INTERNAL COPING

3. What can you do on your own to distract yourself from suicidal thoughts? What do you like to do? What have you done in the past?

EXTERNAL COPING

4.Who can help you cope with your suicidal thoughts?

SAFETY PLAN

5. List your coping strategies from above, starting with the most enjoyable.

6. I agree to remove lethal means from the house. _____ _____ *(Student/Parent/Guardian Intitials)*

PEOPLE TO CALL

7. **Emergency numbers:** I will call if my suicidal thoughts continue to get worse after using the coping strategies listed above.

- Safe and trusted adult: _____

- School personnel: _____

- National Suicide Prevention Lifeline: **1-800-273-TALK (8255)**

- Crisis Text Line: **Text HOME to 741741**

- **911**

8. If no one is available and I have tried all the coping strategies listed above, and I still believe I might do something to end my life, I will go to the emergency room at _____ or call 911.

AGREEMENT

By signing below I agree that I have been part of the creation of this safety plan and that I intend to use it when I am having thoughts of suicide. I realize that my signature below does not make this a legal contract, but rather a plan for my continuesd well-being and happiness.

_____   _____   _____
Student   Signature   Date

_____   _____   _____
School Personnel/Job Title   Signature   Date

_____   _____   _____
Supervisor/Administrator/Job Title   Signature   Date

_____   _____   _____
Parent/Guardian   Signature   Date

*Adapted from Suicide in Schools; *A Practioner's Guide to Multi-Level Prevention, Assessment, Intervention, and Postvention* by Terri A. Erbacher, Jonathan Singer, and Scott Poland

Individual Student Safety Plan

Name: _____   Date: _____

TRIGGERS

1. Think of the most recent suicidal crisis. Write a short description of what triggered the crisis.

school work
thinking about college

SUICIDAL THOUGHTS, BEHAVIORS

2. What are the thoughts, emotions, or behaviors that let you (and those around you) know you were in crisis?

withdrawing
not playing drums

Figure 5.2. Sample Individual Safety Plan. *Source:* Adapted by permission from Taylor and Francis Group LLC Books, *Suicide in Schools: A Practitioner's Guide to Multi-level Prevention, Assessment, Intervention, and Postvention*, by Terri A. Erbacher, Jonathan B. Singer, and Scott Poland, 2015, 220–21.

INTERNAL COPING

3. What can you do on your own to distract yourself from suicidal thoughts? What do you like to do? What have you done in the past?

drumming
play video games

EXTERNAL COPING

4. Who can help you cope with your suicidal thoughts?

my mother
my girlfriend

SAFETY PLAN

5. List your coping strategies from above, starting with the most enjoyable.

> my mother or girlfriend
> drumming
> video games

6. I agree to remove lethal means from the house. ____RB____ ____KLB____ *nt/Parent/Guardian Intitials)*

PEOPLE TO CALL

7. **Emergency numbers:** I will call if my suicidal thoughts continue to get worse after using the coping strategies listed above.

- Safe and trusted adult: __mom cell 987-6543__

- School personnel: __Mr. Smith__

- National Suicide Prevention Lifeline: **1-800-273-TALK (8255)**

- Crisis Text Line: **Text HOME to 741741**

- 911

8. If no one is available and I have tried all the coping strategies listed above, and I still believe I might do something to end my life, I will go to the emergency room at ___ City Crisis Center   II 911.

AGREEMENT

By signing below I agree that I have been part of the creation of this safety plan and that I intend to use it when I am having thoughts of suicide. I realize that my signature below does not make this a legal contract, but rather a plan for my continuesd well-being and happiness.

Rick Bordeaux	Rick Bordeaux	10/9/19
Student	Signature	Date
Dr. Samir/ School Counselor	Dr. Ele Samir	10/9/19
Mrs. Ramirez/ School Principal	Mrs. Ramirez	10/9/19
Supervisor/Administrator/Job Title	Signature	Date
Katherine L. Bordeaux	Katherine L. Bordeaux	10/9/19
Parent/Guardian	Signature	Date

*Adapted from Suicide in Schools; *A Practioner's Guide to Multi-Level Prevention, Assessment, Intervention, and Postvention* by Terri A. Erbacher, Jonathan Singer, and Scott Poland

Chapter Six

Postvention

Tragedy, by its very nature, always catches us off guard. The suicide of a student impacts everyone in the school community. Grief, accompanied by blame, guilt, anger, and confusion, creates an atmosphere of emotional turmoil. Because the death is unexpected, shock makes it hard to know how to react. School leaders must be cautious in how they communicate the story to the school community and to the public.

Awareness of adolescent thinking and behavior should guide the messages that are shared in the aftermath of the death. Regardless of the cause, all student deaths must be treated the same way. To avoid the risk of suicide contagion, share honest information, help students understand the death, and provide strong support to cope with it.

With a prevention plan, schools know how to handle a crisis. Being prepared is like having a guide who helps the community recover and get back on track. If no emergency plan is in place when a suicide happens, resources will most likely not be available to support schools. It makes sense to develop a plan for prevention, crisis response, and postvention before a crisis occurs.

AFTER A SUICIDE: A TOOLKIT FOR SCHOOLS

After a Suicide: A Toolkit for Schools,[1] a free publication by the American Foundation for Suicide Prevention (AFSP) and the Suicide Prevention Resource Center (SPRC), offers best practices and practical tools to help school administrators in the aftermath of a suicide.[2]

The toolkit provides guidance for schools on

• crisis response

- how to help students cope
- working with the community
- working with the media
- memorialization
- social media
- suicide contagion
- bringing in outside help
- going forward

Adapted with permission, the content in this chapter touches on all major topics in the publication. Download the free PDF from either the SPRC or the AFSP website to access the complete toolkit.[3] Templates and additional resources include sample scripts and handouts for each component of the plan.

Crisis Response

News of a student's death often arrives through the grapevine. Confirm the suicide before launching a crisis response. As soon as the facts have been verified, inform the school community of the death, starting with the school staff. Prepare for grief support by helping students and staff cope with their feelings and emotions. Try to maintain normal educational activities as much as possible.

If a school has a Crisis Response Team, there will be a group of professionals ready to step in and take charge immediately. If a school does not have such a team, it is recommended to form one before a crisis occurs. The team of five to fifteen members should include an administrator, counselor, social worker, psychologist, nurse, school resource officer, and other personnel who can remain calm and level-headed during a crisis. Whether the team is districtwide or site based, the lead person acts as the coordinator and point of contact.

Crisis Team Action Plan

Communication

> Who: School officials, deceased student's family, school staff, students, school community.
> What: Fact that a death has occurred. Cause of death—with permission only. Support for family and friends of student.
> When: As soon as possible.
> Where: Staff meeting at school before classes start, students in homeroom classes, parents by letter.

How: Meet in person or small groups. Do not make any announcements through the PA system. Monitor social media accounts. Provide written death notification statement to parents. Give school staff handouts with information about suicide and helping students.

After a Suicide: A Toolkit for Schools includes handouts and sample statements that can be downloaded from the SPRC Resources & Programs webpage:

- Sample Death Notification Statement for Students (including variations for confirmed or unconfirmed suicide death)
- Tips for Talking about Suicide
- Sample Guidelines for Initial All-Staff Meeting
- Sample Death Notification Statement for Parents
- Facts about Suicide in Adolescents
- Youth Warning Signs and What to Do in a Crisis
- Sample Agenda for Parent Meeting
- Key Messages for Media Spokesperson
- Sample Media Statement
- Making Decisions about School-Related Memorials

Schools must react quickly to get ahead of the rumors that spread through social media. If the cause of death is unconfirmed or under investigation, or the family does not want the cause of death disclosed, then only a general factual statement should be issued to the school community. For example, just state that a high school student died and do not mention suicide. If the cause can be shared, explain that suicide has many causes. However, it can be triggered when a young person is deeply distressed or struggling and is often related to underlying painful mental health conditions.

People tend to make personal connections with their own lives if they're feeling vulnerable and may react strongly. Be prepared to offer support. The death is a meaningful opportunity to talk about how to prevent suicide and get help for oneself, friends, or family members.

Sometimes parents don't want the cause of death released because of uncertainty, stigma, or cultural beliefs. Keep in mind, however, that ignoring the issue of suicide increases speculation. Students will talk about it and have questions. Teachers should respectfully note that the cause of death has not been disclosed. But if suicide is brought up, it is appropriate to share accurate information about causes of suicide, ways to prevent it, and how to get help.

Informing the school community must be handled tactfully and acknowledge the family's wishes regarding what they are willing to share. Teachers and staff who knew the student should be told in person. They'll need more information than parent groups or the public. Follow research-based guidelines for safe messaging about suicide to help prevent contagion and avoid dramatizing the student's death. The actual cause of death is always a point of curiosity but should not be a part of the conversation. Focus instead on the student's struggles, including a mental health condition if that was known to be a cause, and how to deal with loss and grief.

The team coordinator is responsible for overseeing all critical tasks. Safety, support for staff and students, and communication with community liaisons top the list, along with any school involvement with funeral plans, the media, and social media. Designated members of the Crisis Response Team (CRT) need to keep track of actions taken and continually monitor activities throughout the school to provide support and resources. They'll meet with school staff and parents to keep them informed.

Safety

Schools should try to follow normal schedules and regular dismissal procedures. Be prepared for parents to call or arrive on campus with questions or concerns. Direct information requests from the media to the designated communication team member. They'll provide a succinct statement for the media and remind them to stay off of school grounds.

Be alert for students who are emotional, withdrawing, or acting out. Have a counselor talk with them privately. Students will naturally congregate in hallways and restrooms to process the news, so be prepared to offer support as needed.

Support for Students and Staff

Arrange for crisis counseling rooms for staff and students. Assign a counselor or other mental health professional to follow the deceased student's schedule. That way they'll be available to respond to questions and give support to classmates and teachers throughout the day.

All students should have the opportunity to meet with counselors as needed. Make roaming substitutes or volunteer teachers available to take over classes for short breaks. Teachers might need to step out for a while or speak with a counselor. Remember that counselors and teachers may be working without breaks to support students. Make food, water, and plenty of tissues available to them.

Be aware of students or staff who may be having extreme difficulty with the loss, especially if they have a history of depression or suicidal thoughts. Offer referrals to community-based mental health professionals if needed.

Community Liaisons

It's helpful to maintain communication with community partners who may be involved in handling the aftermath of a suicide death. Assign a crisis team member as primary contact for each community partner. They'll serve as liaisons responsible for coordinating communication with the police, coroner, medical examiner, and local government officials. Liaisons will also work with community-based mental health and grief support organizations to organize additional support for the school community if needed.

Neighboring school districts can also be an important resource and will often offer to share their counselors to help provide additional support if asked.

Funeral

The team member assigned to share information about the funeral with the school community may need to reach out to the funeral director about the logistics. The service should not be held on the school grounds or during school hours if possible.

The family may not wish to discuss funeral plans with the school liaison. However, it is wise to talk about whether they will allow the people involved in conducting the service to mention the struggles the student was experiencing. It's important to clearly explain that sharing mental health concerns will promote understanding about suicide, reduce stigma, and avoid possible contagion.

As with any death, ask the family's permission to share basic information about the funeral with students, parents, and staff. The liaison can notify the school community of the time and location, and how to express condolences.

If students will be attending the service during the school day, the school needs to follow its normal attendance policy for students and staff. Parents should accompany students planning to go to the service. Arrange for counselors to be present at the funeral so they can be available for support if needed.

Media Relations

Have a media spokesperson on the team respond to all media inquiries. Stick to a simple statement of compassion for the loss of the student. Mention that grief counseling is available and include the timeframe. Notify the media when an informational meeting about suicide prevention for parents and the community has been scheduled, including the time and location. Remind them that cameras and reporters are not permitted on school grounds.

Standard recommendations for reporting on suicide are available for distribution to the media.[4] Because the way the death is portrayed can contribute to suicide contagion if it's sensationalized, it's critical that the media understand the importance of their role in communicating the death of a student appropriately. Media coverage should focus on suicide prevention and mental health issues and avoid covering the method, location, or graphic photos of the death. Ask reporters to include helpful resources, local crisis hotlines, and the National Suicide Prevention Lifeline, 800-273-TALK (8255).

Social Media

Social media can have a tremendous impact on the reaction to a student's suicide, both in negative and positive ways. Controlling the content is virtually impossible, but strategic use of social media tools can help disseminate helpful information and minimize the risk of suicide contagion. Offer support and postvention-oriented messaging. Find and respond to youth who may be at risk and steer conversations in constructive directions.

Assign a social media manager on the Crisis Response Team to ensure cohesive messaging across platforms. School districts with a social media presence have an advantage. They will already have guidelines about how it can be used and platform-specific templates that can be filled out and deployed rapidly in a crisis.

It's best if the social media manager works in partnership with student leaders. Offer assistance and support without trying to take control. Students will know the most popular social media platforms used by their peers. When they come across negative communication that may lead to contagion or endanger at-risk students, they can help guide online conversations into positive messages honoring the deceased student.

Schools can use their own websites along with social media to share information with the school community. Avoid dramatizing or memorializing the loss of life and focus on recovery. Honor the person who died by emphasizing suicide prevention and providing resources and support.

Post details about how students can get help from school counselors or local mental health agencies along with facts related to mental health disorders and the warning signs of suicide. Always include the National Suicide Prevention Lifeline: 800-273-TALK (8255) on every message, as well as the Crisis Text Line: text HOME to 741741. Encourage students to share the information on their own social media pages.

Help Students and Staff Cope with Grief and Loss

Life is an emotional roller coaster for teenagers on a normal day, but the sudden death of a peer is beyond their scope of experience. In the days immediately following the crisis, teachers in every classroom are likely to be involved in helping students process the trauma.

At times it may be best to get back to normal by sticking to lesson plans and focusing on academic topics. But sometimes it's better to talk about what happened. Being open and willing to talk honestly with students about emotions and feelings will help the healing and recovery begin.

Most teachers and administrators, like most other adults, are not comfortable talking about suicide unless they have personal experience with a suicide loss or are trained as counselors. They need tools they can use to guide conversations as they occur.

Give students facts about suicide, without judgment.

- Suicide is often the result of a mental health condition or substance use disorder combined with other life issues that lead to overwhelming emotional and/or physical pain.
- There are effective treatments for people with mental health or substance abuse problems or suicidal thoughts.
- Mental health problems are a health issue. Just as we are not ashamed of having cancer, diabetes, or any other illness, we do not need to be embarrassed or fear seeking treatment for mental health conditions.

The first questions after a suicide are always "Why?" and "What could I have done to prevent it?"

- Know that the person was experiencing extreme pain and distress.
- People who are suicidal often hide their feelings from friends and families, not wanting to be a burden to others or being ashamed of their illness.

Don't focus on the method, but rather on how to cope with feelings and emotions after the loss.

- Focusing on the method can increase the risk to others who may have suicidal ideas.
- Instead of thinking about the death, talk about how the loss has affected everyone.
- Discuss constructive ways to deal with loss and grief: writing in journals, poetry, or letters; art, music; talking with friends about positive shared memories.

Feelings of anger or guilt are common responses.

- Acknowledge the feelings of anger but know that the anger should be directed at the behavior rather than the person who died.
- Understand that we did not recognize the signs because they may have been hidden.

- Despite how well we know someone, we can't always predict their behavior.

Promote help-seeking.

- Seeking help is a sign of strength, not weakness.
- Encourage students to identify a trusted adult to talk to if they or someone they know is feeling worried or depressed.
- Many students think they are "ratting out" their friends if they share their concerns with an adult, but consider the alternative. Would they rather lose a friend or have someone they care about lose their life?

Coping Strategies and Counseling

In a culture of caring, adults in the school community support students by modeling calm, caring, and thoughtful behavior. Giving honest answers to students' questions will go a long way toward dispelling rumors and misinformation. School leaders may find it helpful to have mental health professionals visit classrooms and share information with teachers and students. Counselors and psychologists can start the conversations and suggest coping strategies to help students and staff begin the recovery process.

One size doesn't fit all when it comes to helping students cope with a suicide loss. School counselors, psychologists, social workers, nurses, and if available, community mental health partners, will need to work with students. They can meet in small groups or individually with those who may be at higher risk.

The focus of the groups is to allow students to have a chance to recognize and express their feelings in a safe environment. Beyond knowing they're sad or angry, they will benefit from articulating their concerns and fears and identifying what would make them feel safer. Sharing favorite memories of the student can lift the mood and help students remember positive experiences instead of dwelling on the loss.

Discuss coping strategies to encourage students to shift their attention back to their regular routines and activities. Simple redirection, like participating in favorite activities or hobbies, talking with a friend, reading, going to a movie, or exercising, can help. Remembering how they have coped with difficulties in the past is another simple strategy. Thinking of or writing about people they can turn to for support helps too. Focusing on personal goals and planning for the future without guilt are healthy steps toward recovery.

It's natural for students to want to memorialize the friend they lost. They may be encouraged to do so individually by writing a note to the family, creating a memory book, or writing poetry or in a journal. These are positive ways to express and process feelings.

Include Parents in the Conversation

Parents might be unsure of how to talk about the death with their own children and their friends. Hold a parent meeting and invite them to come. It will give them a safe place to get information and ask questions in person. Since not all parents will be able to attend, post information on the school website along with useful handouts about youth suicide. Encourage parents to contact the school's mental health staff or community mental health providers if they are concerned about their children or other students.

Work Together with Community Partners

In times of crisis, it's important to develop a relationship with other groups that may be involved in the aftermath of a sudden death. Police, local government leaders, funeral home directors, faith leaders, and community mental health providers can be influential in supporting the postvention process. They have unique opportunities to educate community members about suicide as a public health issue. They'll inform their circles of influence about the risk factors that can lead to suicide, warning signs, and resources available for help and support. They can share information on local bereavement support groups of survivors of suicide loss too.

Ask community partners to publicize crisis hotline numbers—the National Suicide Prevention Lifeline: 800-273-TALK (8255) and the Crisis Text Line: text HOME to 741741. Take the opportunity to begin building a community coalition focused on suicide prevention, educating the community, and reaching out to give support to young people in places they gather outside of school.

After a Suicide: A Toolkit for Schools includes specific handouts and links to other resources that will be helpful to community partners. All of these can be downloaded from the SPRC Resources & Programs webpage:

- Support for Survivors of Suicide Loss: A Guide for Funeral Directors
- After a Suicide: Recommendations for Religious Services and Other Public Memorial Observances

How Memorialization Can Lead to Suicide Contagion

It's a natural reaction for grieving students to want to memorialize the deceased. But allowing the memorialization to escalate can glamorize or romanticize the suicide and lead to contagion. Therefore, schools must understand and prevent both issues.

If there are teens who are struggling either with their own issues or because of their relationship with the deceased, the crisis response team must try to find and reach out to those students. Counselors should seek guidance from a mental health professional on whether to use a simple mental health screening tool with all students and, if so, how best to do it.

Recognize the life the student lived without focusing on the death. Include student's friends who are likely to be the most deeply affected by the loss in planning ways to remember the student and acknowledge the loss. Consider the feelings of the student's family and coordinate with them.

Holding a funeral service at the school is not recommended as it will create a permanent connection between the school campus and the death and serve as a constant reminder of the loss. A better option is to encourage the family to hold the funeral after school hours and encourage students to attend with their parents. If the family prefers to hold the service during the school day, students should be allowed to leave campus to attend following the normal protocols for early dismissal. Keep the regular school schedule in place.

Spontaneous memorials created with cards, flowers, poems, stuffed animals, and pictures are likely to pop up on campus. Monitor the messages, but do not dismantle the memorial immediately. Follow up on any messages that seem inappropriate to make sure contributing students are not at risk.

Meet with the students who initiated the memorial to provide an opportunity for them to share their feelings. It also opens the door to discuss the school's concern about glamorizing the death and ultimately leading to possible contagion. Make an agreement to limit the time the memorial is left in place. Five days or the day after the funeral is reasonable. Decide on a plan to gather the memorabilia and either disperse it among the students who want a keepsake or deliver it to the family.

Students know that schools set limits in many situations to keep them safe, but this is not a time to be authoritarian. If students come to school wearing T-shirts or buttons with pictures of the deceased, they may be allowed to wear them for a day, but the staff should explain that others may be uncomfortable seeing constant reminders of the deceased. Suggest alternatives like wristbands with positive statements that may help fill the need of students to express their feelings.

Written memorials, whether online or printed in school yearbooks or newspapers, must also be monitored by adults. Encourage student writers to contribute articles for the yearbook or newspaper that educate others about suicide warning signs and list available resources. Online pages should remain active for only a limited time of up to thirty to sixty days.

If students or the family want to hold an assembly or an event at the school, stick to the guidelines that would be followed after any death. Rather than prohibiting any memorial activities, channel the energy and passion in a positive direction. Plan a fundraiser for a relevant cause or an educational activity that will both honor the life of the student and give hope and tangible solutions for the future.

Request Outside Help

Depending on the circumstances, schools might decide to bring in outside help. Most states have suicide prevention resources that can be found either on the state website or Department of Education site. The Suicide Prevention Resource Center (SPRC) website lists suicide prevention contacts in every state who can assist in finding local experts. There are also national organizations that provide crisis response, postvention consultation, and training. They can put schools in touch with pertinent experts. [5]

MOVING FORWARD

As awareness of the importance of suicide prevention grows, communities across the country are demanding more support. Through legislation at the state level, states are passing laws that encourage or require suicide prevention plans in schools. Regardless of requirements, when programs are initiated after a school has suffered a suicide loss, the tragedy can evolve into an opportunity to educate the school community about warning signs and recovery.

Chapter Seven

Engaging the School Community in Suicide Prevention

When a suicide prevention program is first introduced to the school community, the initial response from teachers tends to be groans. You'll hear exclamations of "Oh, no! Not one more thing to squeeze into an already packed curriculum! I don't have time." Students think something like that will never happen to them and wonder why they should bother to pay attention. Responses from parents are mixed but often stem from the concern that if you talk about suicide, kids will start considering their options and might follow through. Administrators are reluctant to add a distraction that will take time away from academic instruction. If the school community has never been touched by suicide, they may see little value in taking time to prepare for something that isn't likely to happen. Until it does.

Schools that have experienced the suicide of a student will respond much differently. Teachers, students, and parents are invested in learning what they can do to prevent such a painful tragedy from ever happening again. They are ready to join the crusade.

EXPERT COMMENTARY: SANDRA MCNALLY, PREVENTION MANAGER AT EMERGENCY MOBILE PEDIATRIC AND ADOLESCENT CRISIS TEAM-SUICIDE PREVENTION CENTER (EMPACT-SPC) IN TEMPE, ARIZONA

EMPACT-SPC offers nationally recognized suicide prevention programs, including Signs of Suicide and safeTALK, and is a leader in postvention, providing a variety of services to those who have lost a loved one to suicide.

Suicide Prevention in Schools Evolves

> "I believe in prevention. We can make a difference and help youth who are at
> risk."

There's a greater awareness now. Media focus on suicide is increasing.
Schools are more on board. With national as well as state-level groups,
we've really tried to do a good job breaking down the stigma associated with
suicide and help people to feel more comfortable talking about suicide.

Funding has increased, but it goes up and down. It's mostly grants. The
Garrett Lee Smith Memorial Act passed in 2004 after a senator's son died by
suicide, providing some funding for youth suicide prevention. It is instrumental in awarding states and tribes with grant money to use for youth
suicide prevention.

Over the years, doors have opened. People are more willing to talk about
suicide. People see the need for training in suicide prevention and intervention skills. Schools are much more willing to let us come into their arena and
address this issue with their students. Not all schools want a full-fledged
suicide prevention program, but they realize that they need to provide resources to students in crisis. We partner with Teen Lifeline,[1] and many,
many school districts across our county are printing the Teen Lifeline crisis
number on the back of student IDs.

Barriers That Get in the Way

Fear of opening a can of worms. Stigma. Overburdened school counselors
who don't have the capacity to serve as therapists. Time. Figuring out how to
fit it in the school day without taking away from core classes, breaks, testing
times. All of those things. When something isn't completely important or the
number one priority, that's what falls by the wayside. It doesn't fit in, so it
gets put off into the future. Some districts drag their feet even though there's
a clear need. They're just fearful.

How to Face Fear

> "Their fear is that they're going to have all these students running around
> being suicidal and they're not going to be able to handle it."

For example, this one particular school worried that if they showed the *Signs
of Suicide* video and started going into classrooms and talking about suicide,
the resulting mayhem would turn into mad mass chaos! Their fear was students would suddenly become suicidal. There's a fear of the process.

It doesn't work that way. We start by picking just one classroom of thirty
students. We show a presentation that's done professionally using an evi-

dence-based program. All students fill out the screening tool. We look at what the screening tool said, and then we go back and meet with each student individually. If we feel a child is at risk, then we're going to help. We're going to staff the case. We're going to contact the parents to make the referral and recommend they seek help from a mental health professional.

Sometimes there may be a lot of students in crisis or having suicidal thoughts. You want to know that because if you don't, you're not able to help them. Sometimes people think if they don't know, they don't have to do anything about it and they can assume everything is fine and keep their blinders on. Or there might be people working as school counselors who are not comfortable dealing with youth in crisis.

In the school's defense, a lot is put on school counselors and teachers. When suicides happen, schools get blamed. Parents need to do their part and find out what's going on with their children. The school doesn't have a magic wand. We all need to be aware and know the signs of suicide. Everyone should intervene if they see something, not just the school. The school can't magically make children happy. They can't take care of all the problems the students are dealing with. They can only try and make appropriate referrals so students get the help they need.

A lot of schools are in denial. I remember years ago when school principals would say, "We don't have a drug problem on our campus. We don't need these services." I thought, "Are you serious? I guarantee you, some of your students drink or use drugs. You have blinders on if you think you don't have a problem at your school." Suicide prevention is like that now. That's how a lot of schools view suicide until it happens on their campuses. Unfortunately, it's a reactionary kind of thing. Once they have a suicide, then they realize the impact. It's devastating.

What an Effective Model for Suicide Prevention Education Looks Like in Schools

> "If we're not giving opportunities to identify students at risk and making referrals, then we're missing the boat."

Everyone needs to be on the same page. Best practice is to create an opportunity for early identification and referral. That's key with prevention. The awareness piece is great, but it needs to go beyond that. We recommend comprehensive training for the staff, the students, and the parents. That's why we use a program like Signs of Suicide that includes a screening tool to identify students at risk. Students can self-refer, too. Those referrals make a difference.

We shy away from doing school assemblies or things like that. There's no way to individualize. The message is getting out, but then where is the message going? How are we triggering kids with that message? There's no opportunity for them to reach out to get help when they need it.

Getting Buy-In from Principals, Counselors, and Teachers

At the beginning of every semester, we reach out to about a hundred area schools. We give a packet to the school counselor or the principal about all the different programs we can offer them. Then we follow up with the school to ask if they had a chance to look at the information and remind them what we can offer. We go back to the same schools each year to remind them what we're doing. It's a lot of relationship building.

Some schools wait until after a suicide occurs before they realize they need help. Others, because of the media and increased awareness, know they need to learn skills. We allow schools to pick and choose what level of training they want. We build trust with them. When we're on the campus, and they see what we're doing in one area, they're more willing to let the program expand.

One high school, in particular, had a suicide a few years ago on their campus. The school counselors came to our suicide prevention conference that year and just said, "We never want to have this happen again." They got approval from their administration and the whole staff really rallied. Teachers were trained, and the counseling staff is completely on board. That school has had us doing Signs of Suicide[2] every year since. There has not been another suicide on that campus.

When we do the training in schools that have not experienced a suicide, there will be some staff that are really super interested, and some that don't want to be there. And then there are people who have their own issues that play a part in their resistance. Getting complete buy-in is difficult. It depends on the approach.

One district, for example, trained the staff in stages. A good administrator can explain that students come to school with emotional issues and behavioral issues. If they're not addressed, it's going to impede their ability to be successful academically. Helping the whole child makes the teacher's job more effective, so the school leaders started looking at how to help their staff understand some of the challenges that adolescents face today. Then, on staff development days, they introduced the topic of suicide. It wasn't just thrown in their faces but discussed after the staff had more awareness of the many, many challenges that kids today have.

If the administrator approaches it without forethought, it's very apparent. During the training it looks like nobody really cares. Teachers are unengaged and tuned out. It could be that they are just told to stay after school for the training at the last minute. There's no real effort in talking about why this is happening or why it's important.

If we know why something is important or we can see the bigger picture, we're more willing to buy in. Administrators should be asking, "Are you aware of some of the statistics of suicide? Suicide is the second leading cause of death for middle and high school students. Other schools are experiencing suicide deaths, and we don't want this to happen to our students."

Each school is different. Sometimes we can work directly with the counselors and at others the principal has to approve the program. Some need district approval. Then it's trickier to penetrate the layers of bureaucracy. Some school administrators are fearful. They don't want to have a suicide happen at their school. Whatever their motivation is, they're more willing to consider the training than they have been in the past because it's in the media all the time.

How to Initiate a Suicide Prevention Program at Your School or District

The best advice is to go through the proper channels to find out what's allowed or not allowed by the principal or district. Research and find an evidence-based program. Consult with experts in the field for guidance on how to get started—don't wing it. Find another district that has a strong suicide prevention program and learn about their policies and procedures. Put together a committee and create a plan that is manageable in your school or district and safe for students and staff.

A program designed to increase awareness is not enough. The early identification referral process is an important component. There must be a system in place that allows staff to identify students at risk and for students to self-identify. Qualified counselors have to make the necessary referrals. That's effective suicide prevention.

OBSTACLES PREVENTING COMPREHENSIVE SUICIDE PREVENTION PLANS

We avoid talking about things that make us uncomfortable. Suicide is an uncomfortable topic. We find excuses not to get involved in something we don't want to do. Along with the obvious challenges in any school district— time and money—the stigma of suicide allows schools to ignore the issue entirely.

In school districts that have never experienced a suicide loss, getting buy-in from teachers, parents, and administrators at the school and district levels can be challenging. Lack of adequate staffing often proves to be an insurmountable barrier. Few districts have site-based mental health professionals and rely on school nurses and administrators to act as counselors.[3] While the

American School Counselor Association recommends a student-to-counselor ratio of 250 to 1, few states can meet that recommendation. In 2015–2016, Arizona had 903 to 1, and Michigan had 744 to 1. The national average is 464 to 1. Faced with inadequate funding and teacher shortages, hiring additional staff to address mental health is not even on the radar for many school districts.

The flip side of a lack of money is a shortage of time. In schools where the focus is on improving standardized test results, academics take priority during the school day. Any program that impinges on instructional time may be resented or avoided. Think of the school schedule for a typical high school of five hundred to three thousand students. Any change can cause a domino effect with missed instruction having to be made up later.

The stigma of suicide, perhaps the most powerful barrier of all, runs deep. It has afflicted generations of Americans, holding us hostage to shame and fear. School superintendents are likely to balk at even mentioning a suicide prevention plan, worried it will cause parents to rise up in anger. Convinced that suicide prevention education will actually encourage suicide, many parents are passionate in their belief that suicide is a topic best ignored. They insist a prevention program is too intrusive for their children.

Even if a family in the school community has lost a child to suicide, chances are they are too embarrassed and ashamed to admit the cause of death. Fearing the community will judge them for having failed as parents, they choose silence. Very few will advocate for any suicide prevention program for fear of having to share their perceived shame.

HOW TO GET BUY-IN FOR SUICIDE PREVENTION PROGRAMS

Start small. No one can argue the importance of having protocols in place for helping students who show suicidal warning signs or for responding to the suicide death of a student. In fact, schools can be sued if they don't. Failing to get assistance for a student at risk of suicide, adequately supervise that student, or notify parents that their child appears to be suicidal can result in serious legal consequences. School staff, particularly counselors, teachers, and administrators, must know the protocols for those situations both to protect students and avoid possible litigation.

Buy-in for suicide prevention means a willingness to support and participate in a program. Think about who needs to become involved. A different approach for each target group may be necessary. Also, take time to determine the specific goals, which may range from simple awareness of suicide risk to active involvement in a prevention program. Know that it will take time, organization, effort, and patience.

School Connectedness

If there was ever a doubt that creating a culture of caring was a critical component of suicide prevention, consider the research. The CDC reports that school connectedness,[4] the belief that adults and peers in the school care about students' learning and value them as individuals, is an important protective factor. Strengthening school connectedness results in improved academic achievement and healthy behaviors.

Many schools have leaders who focus on creating a positive learning environment for students. But if a school has a high number of discipline problems and frequent turnover in leadership and staff, the culture may not be one of connectedness. Changing and sustaining a school culture is hard. It doesn't happen after one staff meeting or student assembly. It takes strategic planning, time, and effort.

Whether schools choose to use an evidence-based program or design their own model, effective strategies include:

- Professional development and support for teachers and other school staff focused on helping them teach not only academic skills but also social and emotional skills.
- A structured approach to positive classroom management.
- Empowering staff and students by involving them in decision-making activities focused on improving the school culture.
- Creating a variety of opportunities to get parents and families involved in their child's academic learning and school life.
- Building relationships. Finding ways to bring people that don't normally interact together through activities, projects, and programs that require them to talk to each other.

One Step at a Time

Once the concept of building connectedness has been integrated into the school culture, it's easier to take another step forward. Create opportunities for staff and students to learn more about mental health. Educate them on how to support those who may be struggling. School counselors are typically the organizers of mental health events for students, but any administrator, staff member, or student group can take the initiative to get the ball rolling.

- Hold educational events during student lunch hours with information booths and displays focused on health, wellness, and safety issues relevant to teens.
- Invite experts from local mental health organizations. They usually offer giveaways at their booths to attract students so they can initiate conversations with them.

- Schedule information events during Suicide Awareness Month in September. Choose local or national awareness activities. Examples are easily found online. Ask community organizations to share materials and resources.
- Suicide Awareness Month includes World Suicide Prevention Day and National Suicide Prevention Week. Use those activities to launch activities on campus like #BeThe1To.
- #BeThe1To is the National Suicide Prevention Lifeline's message for National Suicide Prevention Month. The phrase can serve as a touchstone for students and remind them to connect with others who may be alone and unconnected.
- Schools can customize the #BeThe1To phrase so it aligns with their efforts to build connectedness.
- The National Action Alliance for Suicide Prevention (Action Alliance) and its partners promote #BeThere messaging to highlight the role the public has in being there for others who might be struggling or in crisis. Use resources from the Action Alliance to help educate students about actions anyone anywhere can take to make someone feel less alone.

Keep the Momentum Going

Keep the conversations going during the weeks following educational events on campus. School connectedness is a powerful theme. It serves as a foundation for going deeper into understanding mental health and making people take notice of students who need help. If you are involved in promoting suicide prevention at your school, your approach should vary depending on which group you are targeting.

Students

- Students are the first to know when one of their friends is struggling. They need tools and training to help them understand how to help.
- Encourage students to organize clubs focusing on building connectedness and supporting others.
- National organizations like Active Minds, Rachel's Challenge, and MindMatters help high school students and staff establish clubs that focus on connectedness along with mental health awareness and support.

Administrators

Because administrators are busy people with a plate full of responsibilities, they have to prioritize. That said, they are likely to agree on the importance of creating a positive school climate and will want to get involved in integrating connectedness into the school culture.

Taking the next step of initiating a suicide prevention program might take some persuasion, though. Ultimately, it is the principal's responsibility to make sure the school is a safe place for students to learn. It shouldn't be hard to convince anyone that a suicide prevention plan is part of school safety.

- Schedule time to meet with administrators and present the facts about youth suicide. Learning that suicide is the second leading cause of death for high school students is shocking. The data about the number of suicide attempts each year is alarming and could be convincing enough to motivate them to take action.
- Request permission to invite an expert in suicide prevention to meet with school administrators. The initial meeting can be scheduled informally in the principal's office. The expert will emphasize the school's critical role in prevention and educate administrators about suicide awareness.
- YouTube videos can be powerful motivators. Look for example online
- Ask the principal for permission to invite an expert to speak to the staff. A guest speaker can be scheduled during a regular staff meeting or in-service day to introduce the topic.
- A discussion following the presentation might be the first time many administrators and staff members have ever talked openly about suicide and its warning signs. The realization that they see students every day who are suffering from undiagnosed and untreated mental illness is eye-opening. Suddenly, certain student behaviors or actions start to make sense.
- Administrators understand that school personnel are obligated to report students who may be at risk. It makes sense to provide teachers with the training they need to spot warning signs and take action.

Teachers

Most teachers are by nature caring and nurturing. But they are busy people and prefer to focus on training and activities that relate directly to their teaching responsibilities. To get initial buy-in, school leaders must provide an incentive to get them involved in "one more thing to do." Teachers are more likely to be engaged if they believe they will benefit personally.

Many states offer recertification or relicensing credit hours for mental health and suicide prevention training. Invite presenters to provide the training on campus to make it easier for teachers to attend. Online classes allow teachers to participate at their convenience. Keep in mind that it will be more meaningful and effective if there are discussions and sharing of ideas among faculty and staff.

- Teachers don't want to be counselors or therapists; they want to teach. If all they are asked to do is identify students who are struggling and refer them to the school counselor, they are willing to take that step.
- The training increases awareness among teachers and referrals to counselors will increase in the weeks following the training.
- Keep the momentum going by scheduling ongoing training on mental health topics, mental health first aid, and suicide prevention.
- Identify teacher leaders and include them in an introductory presentation about youth suicide. Seek volunteers among the group. Ask for help with the prevention planning process, committees such as a suicide prevention program task force, and training for other staff members.
- Include all support staff in school connectedness and suicide prevention efforts. They will often form bonds with students in their roles as instructional aides, nurses, cafeteria workers, custodians, bus drivers, secretaries, and other positions.
- Organize a mentor program to connect adults on campus to students who need additional support.

Parents

Because suicide prevention doesn't just happen at school, parents need to be involved. Getting them to come to the school to learn about any health issue, whether it is drugs and alcohol, mental illness, or suicide prevention is a challenge. Working parents have limited time, and it's normal for them to feel that they can't spare the time to learn about something that does not affect their lives. Turnout is likely to be low when a school or district invites parents to attend an educational presentation of any kind. But the stigma of suicide makes it even harder to get them in the door. So think about times when parents do show up at school and piggyback on top of them. With creative thinking, there are many ways to get parents involved in suicide prevention.

- Most high schools offer freshman orientation events for students and parents. They are often better attended than other academic activities. Since ninth graders are statistically one of the highest risk age groups, it makes sense to include parent workshops on issues affecting teens.
- Middle school orientation activities can be designed along the same lines.
- High school sports draw crowds. While it isn't practical to offer parent workshops during the events, student clubs can take advantage of the opportunity. Promote activities and events that celebrate connectedness, mental health, and wellness. Invite parents and students to attend.
- Entertainment, food, and free child care are effective incentives to get parents on campus. A student performance naturally draws parents to the

school. Feed the families and take care of the little ones. Use the opportunity to encourage parents to attend short workshops following the performance with their middle and high school students on teen issues.

- When traditional methods for getting parents to attend informational presentations aren't effective, don't give up. Just turn up the heat. Parents who are involved in their children's education, working together, create a powerful force for change, but they don't always realize it.
- Identify leaders among parent groups and invite them personally to attend an introductory presentation. The statistics about youth suicide are shocking enough to jolt people into action. Recruit parent leaders as liaisons and arm them with facts. Ask them to bring other parents into the school to learn more about suicide prevention and get those parents involved in spreading the word about the cause too. Parents actively engaged in youth suicide prevention in their community are motivated and get results.

Community Partners

Many states and tribes have suicide prevention coalitions or groups willing to provide support and assistance. Find lists of contacts for your state on the Suicide Prevention Resource Center (SPRC) website. Connect with local mental health organizations and include them in the process of setting up the school prevention program. Reach out to leaders from the ethnic and cultural communities represented in your school. They can help involve students and parents too.

COPY FROM OTHERS

In education, stealing from others is a common practice. "Stealing" ideas about instructional strategies helps teachers learn new skills. The same principle applies to any new initiative. Look for neighboring districts to use as models. Find out about their suicide prevention plans and ask if they're willing to share their experience. Invite them to speak to your school or district administrators about the steps they took to implement a suicide prevention program.

Sharing stories about other schools' programs provides evidence of success and examples of how to overcome obstacles. Those details will prove useful when you're ready to request approval to initiate a suicide prevention plan for your district.

DON'T REINVENT THE WHEEL

Every school is required to have a crisis or emergency plan. Fire drills and lockdown drills are conducted regularly. Although it will function differently, it makes sense to include suicide prevention in each school's emergency or crisis plan. It can be a daunting task to try to create a plan from scratch, but that isn't necessary when there are evidence-based models available for schools to use.

The information on prevention in chapter 4 summarizes the *Model School Policy on Suicide Prevention*,[5] but there are many others to choose from. SAMHSA[6] published the comprehensive *Preventing Suicide: A Toolkit for High Schools* in 2012 that is still relevant today. Several states have created their own suicide prevention models, notably Maine[7] and Montana.[8] Check to find out if your state already has its own model you can use to develop your prevention plan.

Review and distribute copies of your suicide prevention plan with the school community. Make sure all the players have a copy and know how to use it.

TAKE PRIDE IN CARING

In a culture of caring, suicide prevention is an integral part of the school's mission. It is most effective if it is sustained as part of the mental health curriculum or integrated into social skills instruction. Teach students and staff that mental illness is a disease, not a character flaw, and must be treated as one would any other medical health issue.

The goals are simple:

- Prevent suicide.
- Increase awareness and understanding of suicide.
- Improve coping skills.
- Encourage help-seeking behavior.

By initiating a comprehensive suicide prevention plan in your school or district, you are demonstrating the importance of caring for the whole child. You are focusing not only on academic growth but the social and emotional needs that are crucial to student success.

Chapter Eight

Success Stories

WE KNOW SUICIDE IS PREVENTABLE

Suicide is emerging from the shadows as a public health issue that must be addressed. We've come a long way from the days when early efforts created the first suicide prevention centers in the 1950s. Publication of the *National Strategy to Prevent Suicide* in 2012 and work being done by government and nonprofit organizations around the country today are largely responsible for our progress. The statistics don't show a decline in suicides yet. But we know that because of increased awareness and more accurate reporting through the CDC's National Violent Death Reporting System (NVDRS), we have a much better understanding of suicide deaths than in the past.

There are plenty of success stories indicating that we are heading in the right direction. Thanks to a significant shift in the public's perception of suicide, the conversation is changing. Rather than calling someone a coward or blaming them for "taking the easy way out," people are discussing how we can prevent suicides from happening.

Instead of pretending it could never happen to them, educators are talking about suicide prevention in schools. More states are passing legislation to make sure teachers are getting trained in suicide prevention. Many have developed policies and procedures so schools will have plans in place to prevent and respond to suicides.

Materials and resources are readily available to help schools develop their plans and train staff and students. Several states now require mental health curriculum for students. In Virginia, ninth and tenth graders will learn about mental health as part of their health and physical education courses. New York requires schools to address mental health in grades K–12.[1]

States and tribes receiving Garrett Lee Smith grants from the CDC have used actionable data to tailor suicide prevention programs specific to their needs. Funds are used for suicide prevention and improving medical care in all programs that serve youth ages ten to twenty-four.

Outreach to the media about safe reporting by leading experts has been remarkably effective. Reporting of suicides is evolving from sensationalizing the deaths to informing the public about suicide. Newscasters often publish the suicide prevention lifeline number at the end of each story. Even the wording has changed. Reporters no longer say someone has committed suicide, but rather that they died by suicide.

Suicide prevention efforts still have a long way to go to be as easily recognized as the ubiquitous pink ribbons of breast cancer prevention, but attention has mushroomed in recent years. You may have noticed signs and banners for "Out of the Darkness" walks springing up in public parks across the country as more communities host events to support survivors of suicide loss and spread awareness. High schools and colleges are catching on too. Participation in annual suicide prevention week activities each September is growing exponentially.

Advances in suicide prevention in schools are often the result of progress in other areas. When nonprofit organizations and volunteers push their legislators to enact laws and change government policies that support suicide prevention in their communities, it helps schools too. As those changes trickle down to school districts, they enhance student safety.

The National Suicide Prevention Lifeline has added an online chat option to its services. The Crisis Text Line augments that support by providing a text for help number. Schools print those numbers on the backs of their student ID cards to provide support.

INTRODUCTION TO AFSP

Developing best practices for suicide prevention in schools doesn't occur in isolation but as a result of the work of many dedicated people. Those who spend years tenaciously holding on to their goals and sustaining a laser focus make change happen. It is thanks to their efforts that we have so many success stories to share.

Dedicated to research, education, advocacy, and supporting survivors of suicide loss, the American Foundation of Suicide Prevention (AFSP) has been at the forefront of suicide prevention efforts for over thirty years. The organization started with a handful of volunteers and has grown into a major nonprofit. Together with partners from a wide range of other groups inside and outside of government, they advance the knowledge and practice of suicide prevention.

EXPERT COMMENTARY: JOHN MADIGAN, SENIOR VICE PRESIDENT AND CHIEF PUBLIC POLICY OFFICER, AMERICAN FOUNDATION FOR SUICIDE PREVENTION

As the chief public policy officer, John Madigan oversees AFSP's public policy and advocacy programs. He works with state and local officials, legislators, the White House, Congress, and federal agencies on policies that support suicide prevention. He also trains volunteers across the country to advocate for mental health and suicide prevention policies at state and federal levels.

Actionable Data Collection

> "The tipping point has finally occurred. Public officials on the federal, state and local level recognize that between depression, alcohol, and substance use disorder issues, you're looking at 50, 60 million Americans."

One of AFSP's most important areas of focus is researching the causes of suicide. Examination of data from multiple sources—law enforcement, medical examiners, coroners, toxicology, and vital statistics to name just a few—helps to tell a story of a person's life. The details provide clues to factors that lead to death by suicide. Until recently, data collected on suicide deaths was not consistent. Reporting was spotty and unreliable, making meaningful research difficult.

Over the past ten years, the number of states voluntarily submitting data to the National Violent Death Reporting System (NVDRS)[2] has increased. Thanks in part to the persistent efforts of AFSP, the NVDRS is now funded in all fifty states. Getting apple-to-apple information from each of the states about how suicides are completed will be very useful to policymakers. Because they can use state-by-state NVDRS data to determine factors leading to suicide deaths for any age group, researchers studying suicide prevention now have more data to analyze. With increased understanding of suicide, policymakers and advocates will use that knowledge to improve prevention efforts in communities across the county.

It's well known that suicide rates are soaring. Suicide is the tenth leading cause of death in this country and in some states the second leading cause of death for fourteen- to twenty-four-year-olds. But why? If there seems to be a predominance of deaths related to opioid addiction, for example, public officials will be much more aware of what's going on. They know they need addiction services and ways to help people get out of that cycle of addiction and death.

Current data show that suicide rates are increasing the fastest among white men over fifty. Researchers found that in many cases, people carry suicidal ideation they may have had as a teenager or young adult. Later in life, financial concerns or marital issues may become factors leading to suicide. With that knowledge, mental health professionals will be better able to treat suicidal patients and save lives.

Public Safety

The National Suicide Prevention Lifeline, 1-800-273-TALK, is a suicide prevention network of crisis centers that provides a 24/7, toll-free hotline available to anyone in suicidal crisis or emotional distress. A bill was recently passed to look into the possibility of converting the Lifeline phone number into a three-digit number. It would be similar to the 911 emergency system, making it easier for a person in crisis to call for help. AFSP advocates will actively monitor the process while seeking more robust funding for crisis services.

Another important area of focus is gun safety. AFSP initiated a program with the National Shooting Sports Foundation (NSSF) to engage with gun shop owners and create point of sale educational materials. It's not about taking guns away. It's about teaching people that if a family member has a mental health issue, they need to be proactive. A voluntary plan to remove the gun or separate the gun from the ammunition is part of gun safety. Reminiscent of the Mothers Against Drunk Driving campaign, "Friends don't let friends drive drunk," AFSP and NSSF are trying to adopt common-sense approaches.

Funding for Research

Congress recently instructed the National Institute of Mental Health to prioritize suicide prevention research. AFSP is hoping to see funding increase, anticipating the same success advocates for AIDS/HIV research have had. Initially, contracting AIDS/HIV was a death sentence. Because of the dedicated research from the middle 1980s through to the 2010s, what was once a death sentence is now either totally preventable or a manageable chronic illness.

It was accomplished because AIDS activists got a federal law passed back in 1992. Because of the severe nature of this crisis, they would get 10 percent of the total National Institutes of Health (NIH) budget in perpetuity. That's now roughly $3.5 billion a year. It's a great illustration of how the federal government can dedicate the amount of funding necessary for research if they put their mind to it. Of course, suicide is a bit more complicated. But that shouldn't deter us from making a commitment to spending the money necessary to find out what we can do to prevent it.

Grassroots Advocacy

"Quite frankly we're hoping to help hundreds of thousands of people get involved because it's going to take that kind of grassroots activism to move the ball down the field."

In terms of AFSP's advocacy involvement, just ten years ago there was a list of maybe a thousand volunteers. Only a handful of those were engaged and wanted to remain involved. Now there are more than twenty thousand people signed up as part of the field advocate network across the country. Not everyone is active, but that many people can be called on to help when needed. If a bill relating to suicide prevention or mental health is moving in Congress, they'll send emails to their representatives or make phone calls to the committee members in their state senate. Many plan annual organized group visits to their state capitols to meet with legislators. Anyone can sign up to become a field advocate at www.afsp.org/advocacy. There is no cost involved. AFSP hopes to engage hundreds of thousands of Americans interested in becoming part of this grassroots process.

Some of those volunteers meeting with their state legislators build long-term relationships and communicate regularly. As a result, participation among public officials willing and able to take on the issue of suicide prevention at the state level has grown significantly. More and more governors are issuing proclamations designating September as suicide prevention month, and even at the city level, public officials are drawing attention to it.

AFSP volunteers have found strong partners in several state legislative champions. Legislators in a handful of states are not just looking at suicide prevention as a once and done thing, but they're real champions for the cause. They introduce bills every year, get them passed, and go back to bills that were passed a few years ago to improve on them.

Some have shared their personal stories and experiences with suicide. One of the Pennsylvania legislators speaks openly about living with depression and anxiety. He tells how that impacted him as an individual and as a legislator, and what it means for his state. It makes a difference when public figures use their leadership positions to raise the level of awareness in their communities.

Lack of Funds

"Suicide prevention is perhaps the final public health crises to come out of the closet."

Congress is beginning to recognize the need for taking suicide prevention seriously. They're finding funds for research, but major shortages of money for crisis intervention hamper progress. Even though officials understand it's a problem, allocations of funding at the federal, state, and local levels are just not enough. Now that there is more robust suicide prevention research funding, legislators need to start appropriating funds at the federal, state, and local levels to help turn the tide.

For example, the suicide prevention lifeline number, 1-800-273-TALK, has been well publicized, and people are using it to call for help. The calls are routed to crisis centers local to the caller. But federal funding is so limited that there's only enough money to give each crisis center about $1,500. Tragically, crisis centers are closing in many states because they lack financial support.

Not only are crisis centers at risk, but rapid developments in technology change the way people communicate. While many older adults will call the suicide prevention lifeline if they're in crisis, young people are reluctant to pick up a phone to talk. Many prefer to use chat or text features. However, chat services are inconsistently available through the Lifeline, and the text program is totally independent. Efforts need to be undertaken to integrate the successful text program into a comprehensive national crisis network. Increased funding is vital. Ideally, sharing the cost between federal, state, and private sources would make sure everyone involved has skin in the game.

Health Care

Going back to suicide prevention being the last issue to come out of the closet, there's one predominant obstacle slowing progress. Not only are many state officials afraid to put in mandates, but many professional medical organizations don't want to have mandated training on suicide prevention. They feel like they have too many requirements already. Think back to when CPR was not state-of-the-art. Then it became something everyone wanted to get trained on. Or think about the AIDS/HIV movement. All of a sudden, because of the nature of the disease, clinicians and health care workers had to be instructed on how to handle blood products and other fluids. How do we artfully get our medical people to recognize this is not a burden, but something they should relish and think about?

Advocates for mental health say everybody needs an annual checkup from the neck up. But with the burden on the medical community, there's a dearth of mental health care providers. Many of the current providers don't accept insurance because they're small business people. If you can get someone to pay you $200 in cash for 45 minutes, versus a $93 reimbursement from an insurance company, who are you going to choose as your patient? That practice limits access, obviously.

There are other institutional and structural issues that must be addressed at federal, state, and local levels as we move ahead. For example, reimbursement, the bundling of service payments, and issues of legal liability. Medical providers are concerned that if they start asking patients if they are suicidal, and some actually complete suicide, their families might come back and sue them.

Urgency

If a football program is viewed as being essential to a school district, why isn't a mental health program viewed as being essential? How do we make public officials understand that mental health and suicide prevention has to be a priority, much like they've determined for cancer, HIV/AIDS, and Alzheimer's? We have to make people understand what's going on and take action.

STORIES OF SUCCESS

If you keep an eye out, you'll notice there are stories about suicide prevention with positive outcomes all around us. Find stories about hope and recovery like this one on the Suicide Prevention Lifeline website.[3] Mathew had just started college, expecting his time there to be the best year of his life. Instead, he suffered from severe depression. Not wanting to burden friends and family, he told no one. After enduring six months of increasingly dark thoughts, he finally reached out to friends for help. Surprised that instead of judgment or ridicule, he got support and help for his illness, Mathew was inspired to tell his story to help others. His message is one of hope and encouragement, and the importance of speaking out to tell friends and loved ones when you are struggling. He encourages others to chat with the National Suicide Prevention Lifeline online or call them at 1-800-273-TALK (8255).

Some people wonder whether a phone call to a support line such as the National Suicide Prevention Lifeline can actually save a life. There is plenty of evidence supporting positive outcomes. Many studies are based on anecdotal evidence, like the story that vividly describes a writer's path through the torture of severe depression. Her call to a suicide prevention hotline saved her life.[4] Others are based on hard data. A study about data from 550 callers found that when crisis centers provide follow-up care to suicidal callers, results are even more effective. The vast majority of callers believed the intervention stopped them from killing themselves.[5]

Successful Interventions

Results from several studies reveal interventions that work. One study on youth-nominated support teams tracked suicidal adolescents after they had been hospitalized. Each teen selected a caring adult to support them. That adult was trained in suicide prevention and received assistance from support staff. The teens were followed along with a control group without support for eleven to fourteen years. Not surprisingly, there was only one suicide death among the group of 223 teens with support from a caring adult. The control group of 225 lost thirteen, either by suicide or drug-related deaths.[6]

Another study, the Safe Alternatives for Teens and Youth (SAFETY) study, examined family treatment as an intervention for suicidal youth. Two therapists trained in cognitive and dialectical behavior therapy worked with families, one with the child and the other with the parents. The study found that participants had a significantly higher probability of survival than those who received other treatment.[7] A different study on dialectical behavior therapy for suicidal adolescents found it to be more effective than other forms of therapy within the first twelve months of treatment.[8]

The school-based prevention program Signs of Suicide (SOS) has been mentioned in several different chapters of this book. Along with teaching students to identify the warning signs of suicide risk and seek help from adults, a depression screening tool is available for schools to administer. Researchers measured the number of self-reported suicide attempts before the program started and again three months after, then compared results with students who had not participated. Results showed a significant decrease in the number of students reporting a suicide attempt. They also showed that teens had greater knowledge of depression and were more likely to get help for themselves or a friend.[9]

Kidpower, an organization that teaches safety to children and adults, shares a success story about how a teenager used social media to intervene with a suicidal friend. During an online chat, the friend revealed she planned to kill herself. The teen was able to convince her friend to call a suicide prevention lifeline. As a result, the friend received counseling and support.[10]

Actionable Data and Research

The National Violent Death Reporting System (NVDRS) provides states and communities with a clearer understanding of violent deaths. At first glance, the idea of collecting data about violent deaths seems morbid. But when you dig deeper, you realize that putting together facts about a specific incident from different sources can often lead to understanding the why.

The first step is pooling all the information from different sources including death certificates, coroner/medical examiner reports, law enforcement reports, and toxicology reports. Adding an examination of circumstances that lead to suicide helps researchers form a bigger picture of the possible causes of suicide deaths. That might include depression or other mental illness along with stressful relationships or financial problems. Combining data from multiple deaths translates into critical information for creating effective prevention programs and policies.

Utah, having one of the country's highest suicide rates, used their state Violent Death Reporting System (UTVDRS) to compare data about homicides and suicides.[11] A study found that suicides accounted for 83 percent of violent deaths, but they were rarely mentioned by the media. In contrast, 79 percent of local news articles focused on homicides.

Based on that data, the Utah Department of Health developed a Suicide Awareness Kit for media. The toolkit includes fact sheets about the scope of the problem, risk, and protective factors, and strategies for preventing suicide. Armed with data and guidance on appropriate reporting on suicide, members of the local media learned to report on suicide deaths in ways that inform and educate the public about suicide prevention without sensationalizing the stories.

Translating data into action, Wisconsin used results from the Wisconsin Violent Death Reporting System (WVDRS) to increase prevention efforts and make improvements in mental health services.[12] In addition, they worked to inform the public about means reduction through firearms safety training that emphasized safe storage of weapons.

WVDRS data was also used to launch the Wisconsin School Mental Health Project, a program implemented in over twenty-five school districts. Targets included preventing suicides by reducing the stigma of mental illness, training adults to recognize students at risk, and helping students and their families access mental health services.

Advocacy

It is amazing how much impact a small group of people can have. If you are passionate enough about your cause to invest time and energy, you can influence legislators to pass legislation that will make your state and nation safer. Look to the American Foundation for Suicide Prevention (AFSP), the National Alliance on Mental Illness (NAMI), and other nonprofits for guidance. They have developed a range of programs to organize and train volunteers eager to advocate for mental health legislation in their communities and in Washington, DC.

As a direct result of the efforts of advocacy volunteers in recent years, almost all states have passed legislation that addresses suicide prevention in schools.[13] Statutes range from very prescriptive to mere suggestions. Some allow certified teachers and administrators to earn continuing education credits for suicide awareness and prevention training. Others require annual training for all public school nurses, teachers, counselors, school psychologists, administrators, and social workers. Several states have even funded a position for a state prevention coordinator to carry out training programs.

Health education has been on the back burner for schools hard-pressed for time to meet all the academic standards. However, awareness of the importance of mental health and social-emotional learning is growing. Several forward-thinking legislatures now require mental health curriculum or suicide prevention instruction for students in elementary, middle, and high schools.

Have you ever considered advocating for change? You have the power to influence policymakers. Anyone can become an advocate for a cause they feel passionate about. If you want to play an active role in making schools safer for students, speak up and voice your concerns. Join or form a group of like-minded educators for greater impact. The most successful advocates stay involved over time and build relationships with their legislators and community leaders. Persistence pays off in positive results.

To get involved in suicide prevention efforts at local, state, or national levels, look for advocacy opportunities available through established organizations.[14] The American Foundation for Suicide Prevention (AFSP) has a highly successful Field Advocate program that recruits, trains, educates, motivates, organizes, and supports teams representing their communities. Participants learn how to educate and influence public officials about policies affecting suicide prevention.

NAMI offers resources on its website for anyone who wants to advocate for mental health. Along with identifying your legislators, they provide simple templates to send messages and share your concerns. Current issues are posted on the site informing NAMI advocates which topics are active in mental health public policy legislation.

Educators have access to National Education Association (NEA) resources on the Advocacy Resources for Suicide Prevention page of the NEA website. A brief overview of suicide prevention and resources available for schools provides talking points. The NEA encourages teachers to get involved by advocating for improved suicide awareness and prevention efforts in their own school districts and communities.

Advocacy doesn't have to be political. Start by educating yourself on current mental health and suicide prevention efforts. Attend local training like Question, Persuade, and Refer (QPR) or safeTALK. If there are suicide prevention groups or chapters in your area, participate in their activities.

AFSP and NAMI have a presence in many cities and towns. Use your knowledge and connections to advocate for suicide prevention education in your community.

Education

Legislation that requires training for teachers in suicide prevention makes sense. Because teachers spend so much time with children, they must act *in loco parentis*. They assume parental status and responsibilities for children while they are in their care. Since those responsibilities include keeping their students safe, it's important to know how to recognize warning signs and take action.

There are far more options for training now than in the past. Administrators in states with suicide prevention coordinators can schedule training directly through their education agencies/departments. In places where prevention policies are just emerging, local and national suicide prevention organizations will often provide experts to work with teachers, students, and parents at no cost to the schools. Free online courses are also available.

Suicide prevention awareness efforts have been successful in educating the public about warning signs and informing communities that suicide is preventable. Simply publishing the Suicide Prevention Lifeline and Crisis Text Line numbers to accompany every story about suicide death means help is more accessible to those at risk.

Survivors of suicide loss often find themselves deeply involved in suicide prevention efforts as part of their healing process. Through their participation with national and local prevention organizations, they emerge so well informed that they become resources for others. Many go on to become advocates for mental health legislation or presenters for schools in their communities.

Language

Through education and awareness campaigns, the way people talk about suicide is changing. The vocabulary we use to talk about suicide and prevention affects public perception. Think about the death of Robin Williams, a highly respected actor and comedian. When you heard about that tragedy, did reporters say he died by suicide? Or did they say he committed suicide? The latter response seems negative and judgmental. The first is simply a statement of fact. Thanks to guidelines published for the media,[15] stories have shifted away from sensationalizing a suicide death. You may have noticed that most stories about suicide are now followed by a listing of the suicide prevention lifeline. They often include encouragement to seek help if you or someone you know is struggling.

Calling someone a coward or blaming them for "taking the easy way out" is hurtful. Promoting awareness about the causes of suicide teaches people to understand that suicide is far from an easy way out. We can also change the way we talk about mental illness. Remember that just because a person has a diagnosis, they are not their disease. Rather than saying a person is a schizophrenic or bipolar, we are learning to say they have schizophrenia or a bipolar disorder. We can describe a person with a mental illness as having a mental health disorder, condition, or problem. It makes the illness sound more like a physical health issue without the negative connotation of a mental deficiency.

CONCLUSION

We need only to look at numbers to see the suicide rate has been climbing in recent years. The opioid drug crisis, social media, pressure on students to perform well, and loneliness among older adults have all contributed. However, if you are an optimist, you might wonder if the higher numbers may also be a result of increased awareness and willingness to openly discuss suicide. Historically, suicide deaths have been underreported. Maybe the stigma is finally loosening its grip, and as we learn more about the causes of suicide, we can also celebrate our prevention efforts for every life saved. The more people get involved, the bigger the suicide prevention movement will grow. So spread the word. Make a difference. Be there.

Chapter Nine

What the Future Will Be

You and I have the ability to influence the future. Our daily lives are inundated with constant noise from the 24-hour news cycle and social media. We are surrounded by the drama, tragedies, disasters, and adversity that shape our world every day. If we don't limit what we pay attention to, it can feel overwhelming. One way to gain control is to take action and get involved in a meaningful cause that will make a positive difference.

Busy people have so many responsibilities it may seem impossible to take on one more. But for those whose lives have been touched by suicide or want to be part of the solution, advocacy is a powerful tool for change. It can be very fulfilling and helps to heal the pain of loss. The act of increasing awareness to help prevent suicide, raise funds for research, or offer comfort to survivors of suicide loss gives our lives meaning and hope.

Getting involved in suicide prevention can be scary for educators, often because they don't want to do it alone or they never acted as a voice for a particular cause before. Sometimes all it takes is to make the first move. Prevention organizations always need volunteers, so a logical starting place is to explore their websites and pick one that resonates. [1]

Even if you prefer not to become actively involved, be an advocate for student safety and share what you know about suicide prevention with others. Increasing awareness one person at a time will cause a ripple effect.

EXPERT COMMENTARY: DOREEN MARSHALL, VICE PRESIDENT OF PROGRAMS AT THE AMERICAN FOUNDATION FOR SUICIDE PREVENTION (AFSP)

Known for its research, advocacy, and education programs, AFSP raises awareness, funds scientific research, and provides resources to those affected by suicide. As the vice president of programs, Doreen Marshall oversees all AFSP education and loss and healing programs. The wide range of research-based programs developed by AFSP includes training in mental health and suicide prevention for schools.

Suicide Prevention in Schools

"We're in better shape now with suicide prevention in schools than we've been at any point in the past."

With more schools training their teachers and staff, suicide prevention efforts are a lot better now than ever. There's a real focus on making sure gatekeepers within the school community have some knowledge about prevention. Schools develop specific suicide prevention policies and know what to do.

AFSP partnered with several other organizations to develop the *Model School District Policy on Suicide Prevention*,[2] a document that helps guide schools in developing their suicide prevention policies. In collaboration with the Suicide Prevention Resource Center (SPRC), AFSP also provides *After a Suicide: A Toolkit for Schools*[3] to help schools respond to a suicide death within their school community. Having those kinds of resources to guide schools plus legislative efforts in many states like mandating suicide prevention training of teachers and other staff have made a real difference.

It's Safe to Talk about Mental Health and Suicide

"If you're trying to protect young lives, you can't ignore suicide prevention as a part of safety education."

Because more students are coming to school with mental health concerns, the curriculum is expanding to include mental health. Along with a growing awareness in schools that suicide is a leading cause of death for young people, the public has become more knowledgeable. The conversation has changed from a time when people were afraid or ashamed to mention suicide to the realization that talking about it helps us to address it. As long as we discuss it responsibly using safe messaging guidelines and are mindful of age-appropriate information, there's no danger. In fact, having these open conversations gives us a better chance at prevention.

Also, public perceptions of suicide and mental health are shifting to be more in line with what we know through science. More people now believe suicide is preventable. We still have a long way to go in terms of general education about suicide prevention and mental health for the public, but we've made substantial progress over the last ten years. Fortunately, the current generation is much more open about mental health. There's a willingness to share feelings, often evidenced through social media. Those changes are leading to more dialogue about mental health in ways that can't be ignored.

From the advocacy standpoint, suicide loss survivors are leaders of the charge to open the public dialogue about suicide as a health concern. Those efforts are being joined by others impacted by suicide. No longer limited to just those who have lost loved ones, many people see themselves as having a stake in suicide prevention in their communities.

Components of an Effective Suicide Prevention Model for Schools

"The best setup is one where the teachers, the parents, and the community are all working in tandem, and where there's a culture at the school that promotes help-seeking."

My first recommendation is that schools use research-based suicide prevention gatekeeper training programs. Teachers and staff should be trained in suicide prevention and warning signs. They need to be familiar with the school's policy and procedures on how to address a student who has been identified as at risk. Both of those components are needed regardless of what specific education program is chosen.

Many schools have a crisis plan, and while suicide may be incorporated into it, suicide prevention deserves its own attention. Schools that follow recommendations for best practices publish clear policies related to suicide prevention that also addresses suicide postvention. The school staff has to be knowledgeable. Not only about warning signs and risk factors but also about what to do if they get information that a student might be struggling or suicidal. If a student is in crisis, teachers and staff need to know how to find help within the school. Because of their training, school counselors and licensed school mental health professionals play a different role than teachers and will provide support for students and staff.

The notion that students are encouraged to seek help no matter what they're struggling with, whether academics or mental health, is not unique to suicide prevention. The best setup is one where teachers, parents, and the community are all working in tandem, and there's an environment at the school that promotes help-seeking. It needs to be infused in the culture of the school. Also, when schools encourage students to seek help, they need to make sure they're getting the right help. It's important for students to know that trusted adults are accessible and welcoming and will know what to do if a student is struggling.

Schools with strong gatekeepers, effective parent-teacher and community collaboration on student mental health, and clear policies tend to have effective suicide prevention programs. Adequate mental health support and knowledge of community mental health resources and providers are also critical. Help-seeking among the student body and a culture where it's smart to get help for mental health concerns need to be the norm. When all of those things are in place, it works.

Help-Seeking Behavior Is Key

"Promoting help-seeking is a way to be upstream. You start before you have a crisis or before you have a death."

There is a growing realization that while a school may not experience a suicide death, they are likely seeing students who have had thoughts about suicide or who may have attempted. Data from the Youth Risk Behavior Survey and other surveys on student well-being and mental health concur. Alarming numbers of students consider making a suicide attempt each year. Because these students are interacting with others at school every day, it makes sense to promote help-seeking. Schools need to develop a culture where it's smart to get help for mental health concerns.

While suicide prevention education at the elementary level is uncommon, there has been an increase in integrating programs that promote emotional expression and emotional regulation at younger ages. When schools implement upstream approaches in the elementary grades, it's easier to address suicide because there's already a foundation for introducing conversations about mental health.

Because they spend time with students, teachers are in a position to observe and identify youth who exhibit warning signs and at-risk behaviors— even when they don't ask for help. However, they can't be expected to act as frontline mental health care providers because they're not trained for that. Schools must make sure that teachers understand who to seek out for assistance if they become concerned about a student.

That said, providing mental health care to students who need it can be a challenge. Unfortunately, there may not be enough mental health personnel for the number of students in many schools and districts. When a student is identified as at-risk, access to mental health assessment and care at school and within the community can become an issue. The school's effort to help connect the student to quality treatment may be limited if the community doesn't have services readily available. Schools are often caught in a shifting line between where the school's responsibility for a student starts and stops. Ideally, parents and others in the community act as partners to support student mental health.

Social-Emotional Learning and Mental Health Education

> "There's a movement toward seeing mental health conditions just like other health issues that sometimes require treatment or intervention."

There are programs available for schools that address emotional expression and emotional regulation. The PAX Good Behavior Game[4] has demonstrated effectiveness with students in the primary grades. AFSP's More Than Sad program is focused on detecting depression and anxiety to reduce suicide risk and promote help-seeking among students and their peers.

There is strong evidence that cognitive behavioral skills and dialectic behavioral therapy (DBT) skills can be very effective with emotional regulation, anxiety, and depression. Researchers at the University of Washington, psychologists Jim Mazza and Liz Dexter-Mazza, have done some work on suicide prevention in schools by incorporating DBT skills into school-based learning. They developed effective programs that blend those skills into student learning about mental health and expression of emotions.[5]

It's smart to teach children those skills early. They need to learn and apply them both inside and outside of the school environments before they experience a mental health episode or suicidal thoughts.

Advances in Suicide Prevention

In states where mental health support is improving, we see increases in efforts toward mental health education, mental health awareness, and better access to quality mental health care. This progress helps schools feel more confident that if they train teachers to identify struggling students, there will be access to adequate, evidence-based care.

It can be very hard to get psychiatric care, and there are long wait times for available appointments. When people can't access a psychiatrist, they often see their primary care doctor for treatment of mental health concerns. Some of the current initiatives at AFSP include training those providers in mental health care. Since primary care physicians, pediatricians, and ob-gyns are increasingly likely to be in contact with those at risk for suicide, training them in prevention strategies is a logical step.

> "Roughly half of all suicide deaths are by firearm, so we are looking at firearm education initiatives which also impact students."

AFSP's Project 2025 is a strategic initiative to reduce the suicide rate 20 percent by the year 2025. We are focusing on policies and procedures that help reduce risk in four areas within Project 2025: the criminal justice system, emergency departments, large health care systems, and firearms. Prevention education in the four focus areas will affect large groups of people across all age groups. It will help to reduce suicide if folks in each of those settings get adequate care, have their risks detected and treated, and learn about safety planning.

Another area of focus within the suicide prevention movement is improving treatment for people living with mental health concerns. Unfortunately, there's still a considerable societal stigma against people who experience suicidal ideation or attempts in their past. Including those with "lived experience" of suicidal ideation helps suicide prevention efforts and promotes recovery. Through education, people are starting to understand that with treatment, they can recover and lead productive lives.

How to Initiate a Suicide Prevention Program in Your School or District

> "Overall, anything that a school can do to promote a help-seeking climate within the student body will help."

Start by using resources like the *Model School Policy* and the *After a Suicide* toolkit. Evaluate existing policy and procedures or develop a suicide prevention policy and procedures if they do not currently exist. AFSP has chapters in fifty states, and we encourage schools to reach out to their local AFSP chapter for assistance.

Our chapters can provide the More Than Sad training, often at no cost to schools, and share other suicide prevention resources. More Than Sad has training components for teachers and school staff, high school students, and parents. AFSP also has a program called Signs Matter: Early Detection,[6] a K–12 teacher training for suicide prevention developed in partnership with Legal One and Rutgers Behavioral Healthcare. This low-cost training for school personnel is online and can be completed individually and discussed as a group.

In a school that promotes a help-seeking climate, adults are accessible and talk openly with students about mental health. Another program called Sources of Strength[7] is one that schools have used to promote help-seeking behavior utilizing peer support. It's based on a peer leader model since students often turn to other students when in distress.

It's important that schools do not leave parents out of the equation in their suicide prevention efforts. Make them partners in this process. Bring training to them and listen to their concerns. All of that will help suicide prevention efforts.

If a school does experience a suicide, it needs a comprehensive postvention plan. When a suicide happens in a school community, people don't understand how to talk about it. They're not sure how to provide support for those who have been impacted. In the absence of knowing what to do when they hear of a suicide death, schools often don't do anything in response. That's why we have resources like the *After a Suicide* toolkit to help them. If a school experiences a suicide death, it's important that it addresses the death in a way that sends the right message to students and faculty. Providing support and resources to those affected by suicide loss can also help with prevention efforts moving forward.

We are experiencing a very encouraging time in suicide prevention. Even though we're not seeing the numbers of annual deaths decline yet, we have more research and better reporting systems to help us understand the problem. More is happening now in the field of suicide prevention in general, but especially in schools. We are starting to see the tide shift. The more we do, the more we're going to see our collective efforts having an impact on suicide.

HOPE FOR THE FUTURE

Hope is perhaps the most powerful tool available. The belief that we can change the way things are through persistence and perseverance means we will never give up. Based on where we are now, we know what to focus on next to continue our battle to prevent suicide and save lives.

- Teach resilience. When you think about protective factors, resilience is key. Yet how many teachers and parents intentionally teach children how to be resilient?
- Mental health education K–12. A comprehensive mental health curriculum cannot be optional. It is as important as language arts, math, science, and social studies.
- Development of quality instructional materials.
- States need to create standards in mental health that are relevant in today's world for all grade levels. They must prepare children for a future in which mental health and physical health are addressed equally.
- Publishers who take time to develop and market effective mental health instructional materials will provide an important service to students and teachers.

- A culture of caring. Fortunately, there are quality programs already available to teach children positive behavior skills and to build a culture of caring in every classroom. Positive Behavioral Interventions and Support (PBIS), a federally funded program, is designed to improve social, emotional, and academic outcomes for all students.[8] Responsive Classroom is an evidence-based approach to teaching that focuses on engaging academics, positive community, effective management, and developmental awareness.[9]
- Stop the stigma. Start talking about health from the shoulders up, not just from the shoulders down. Teach children that when they ask for help, things will get better. But only if you also give teachers and parents the skills to respond the right way to those requests and take action when needed. All educators need to know risk factors, recognize warning signs, genuinely care about the health and safety of their students, and take action.
- The whole child perspective is not a new idea but can be a nebulous, intangible concept. Funding is now available to help schools to actively address it. Title IV, Part A, is a federal grant that promotes integrating social-emotional learning and mental health into the academic curriculum through the Safe and Healthy Students component.
- Join the National Alliance on Mental Illness (NAMI) StigmaFree campaign.[10] Each of us has the power to influence the way those around us view mental health. We must not fear openly discussing mental health issues. By facing the stigma head on, we can stop shame and embarrassment from trapping those who are struggling in silence, preventing them from seeking help.
- Be an evangelist for suicide prevention in schools. Be the voice. Teach others what you know and support them in their efforts to prevent suicide. Together we can make the world safer for our children.

Chapter Ten

Resources

PREVENTION: GUIDEBOOKS AND TOOLKITS

American Association of Suicidology. "Guidelines for School-Based Suicide Prevention Programs." http://www.sprc.org/sites/sprc.org/files/library/ aasguide_school.pdf.

American Foundation for Suicide Prevention and Suicide Prevention Resource Center. *After a Suicide: A Toolkit for Schools.* http://www.sprc.org/sites/sprc.org/files/library/AfteraSuicideToolkitforSchools.pdf.

Centers for Disease Control and Prevention offers an assortment of resources and tools relating to coordinated school health, school connectedness, and health and academics. http://www.cdc.gov/healthyyouth/schoolhealth/index.htm.

Family Acceptance Project. "Supportive Families, Healthy Children: Helping Families with Lesbian, Gay, Bisexual & Transgender (LGBT) Children." http://familyproject.sfsu.edu/publications.

Maine Youth Suicide Prevention Program. *Youth Suicide Prevention, Intervention, and Postvention Guidelines: A Resource for School Personnel.* 2009. http://www.maine.gov/suicide/docs/Guideline.pdf.

Model School District Policy on Suicide Prevention: Model Language, Commentary, and Resources—published by the American Foundation for Suicide Prevention in collaboration with the American School Counselor Association, the National Association of School Psychologists, and the Trevor Project—gives educators and school administrators a comprehensive way to implement suicide prevention policies in their local community. Refer to the second edition published in 2019 for the most current guidance.https://afsp.org/our-work/education/model-school-policy-suicide-prevention/.

Montana Crisis Action School Toolkit on Suicide (CAST-S 2017) was created to meet state requirements. It is a comprehensive document that can serve as a model for other states seeking to develop a suicide prevention policy tailored to their specific needs.https://dphhs.mt.gov/Portals/85/suicideprevention/CAST-S2017.pdf.

National Center for School Crisis and Bereavement (NCSCB) offers education materials, as well as comprehensive expert consultation and training for school professionals and communities preparing for or responding to crisis events. The center also offers support for policies that encourage best practices in crisis and grief support in schools and research in the fields of childhood bereavement and disaster preparedness. https://www.school crisiscenter.org/help-me-prepare/.

U.S. Department of Health and Human Services Substance Abuse and Mental Health Services Administration Center for Mental Health Services. "Preventing Suicide: A Toolkit for High Schools." https://www.store.samhsa.gov/product/Preventing-Suicide-A-Toolkit-for-High-Schools/SMA12-4669.

SCHOOL PROGRAMS

American Foundation for Suicide Prevention. "More Than Sad: Suicide Prevention Education for Teachers and Other School Personnel." https://afsp.org/our-work/education/more-than-sad/.

NE Prevention Resource Center. "American Indian Life Skills Development/Zuni Life Skills Development." http://www.humanserviceagency.org/NEPrevention/index.php/american-indian-life-skills-development.

Suicide Prevention Resource Center. https://www.sprc.org/settings/schools.

Screening for Mental Health, Inc. "Signs of Suicide Prevention Program (SOS)." http://www.mentalhealthscreening.org/programs/youth-prevention-programs/sos/.

The Trevor Project. "Lifeguard Workshop Program." https://www.thetrevorproject.org/education/lifeguard-workshop/.

CRISIS SERVICES FOR STUDENTS

Crisis Text Line is a free text message service providing 24/7 support to those in crisis. Text HOME to 741741.

National Suicide Prevention Lifeline is a 24-hour, toll-free suicide prevention service available to anyone in suicidal crisis or their friends and loved ones. Call 1-800-273-TALK (8255). Callers are routed to the closest possible crisis center in their area. Online chat is also available on their website. http://www.suicideprev entionlifeline.org.

TrevorChat is a free, confidential, secure instant messaging service that provides live help to lesbian, gay, bisexual, transgender, and questioning young people ages thirteen to twenty-four. https:// www.thetrevorproject.org/get-help-now/.

TrevorLifeline is a nationwide, around-the-clock crisis intervention and suicide prevention lifeline for lesbian, gay, bisexual, transgender, and questioning young people ages thirteen to twenty-four. Call 1-866-488-7386. https://www.thetrevorproject.org/get-help-now/.

TrevorText. Confidential text messaging with a Trevor counselor, available 24/7/365. Text START to 678678. https://www. thetrevorproject.org/get-help-now/.

SUICIDE PREVENTION ORGANIZATIONS AND PROGRAMS

American Association of Suicidology (AAS) is a nonprofit association dedicated to the understanding and prevention of suicide.http://www.suicidology.org/.

> *School Suicide Prevention Accreditation Program.* Training for school psychologists, social workers, counselors, nurses, and other school personnel. https://www.suicidology.org/training-accreditation/school-accreditation-program/.

American Foundation for Suicide Prevention (AFSP). AFSP develops evidence-based programs using the latest science on suicide prevention. They offer a range of prevention training programs available through local AFSP chapters or from their online store. https://afsp.org or https://stores.kotisdesign.com/afspexternal.

> *It's Real: College Students and Mental Health.* A documentary film featuring real stories and experiences about mental health issues.
>
> *Mental Health First Aid Training: Youth Mental Health First Aid Training.* An eight-hour course that teaches participants to assess a situation, select and implement interventions, and secure appropriate care

for the individual. This course is offered by other organizations as well.

Model School District Policy on Suicide Prevention. A model schools and districts can use to implement suicide prevention policies.

More Than Sad. Program that teachers, teens, and parents can use to recognize depression and seek help.

Signs Matter: Early Detection. Online training for K–12 educators.

Talk Saves Lives: An Introduction to Suicide Prevention. Community-based presentation that introduces suicide prevention.

The Jason Foundation, Inc. (JFI) is dedicated to the prevention of the "silent epidemic" of youth suicide through educational and awareness programs that equip young people, educators/youth workers, and parents with the tools and resources to help identify and assist at-risk youth. http://jasonfoundation.com/.

B1 Program. Information, tools, and resources to teach students to be aware of youth suicide, how to respond to a friend in trouble, and how to act.

Coaches Assistance Program. A program to teach coaches and other athletic department personnel to recognize signs and symptoms of suicide.

Curriculum Kit. A youth curriculum unit for the awareness and prevention of youth suicide.

A Friend Asks. A free smartphone app that provides the information, tools, and resources to help a friend who may be struggling with thoughts of suicide.

Professional Development Series. Staff development modules on awareness and prevention of youth suicide.

Seminar for Parents and Community. A youth suicide prevention seminar for parents and communities.

The Jed Foundation (JED). Transitioning into adulthood can bring big changes and intense challenges. The Jed Foundation empowers teens and young adults with the skills and support to grow into healthy, thriving adults by protecting emotional health and preventing suicide. Most programs are designed for colleges and universities. Those listed below are suitable for high school students. www.jedfoundation.org.

13 Reasons Why Talking Points. Tips for viewing and discussing the Netflix series based on a popular novel by the same name.

Set to Go. A program that guides students, families, and high school educators through the social, emotional, and mental health challenges related to the transition out of high school to college and adulthood.

National Alliance on Mental Illness (NAMI) is the nation's largest grassroots mental health organization dedicated to building better lives for the millions of Americans affected by mental illness. www.nami.org.

> *NAMI Ending the Silence.* A presentation that helps audience members learn about the warning signs of mental health conditions and what steps to take when symptoms of a mental illness are observed in themselves or others. The presentation includes components for students, school staff, and parents.

National Center for the Prevention of Youth Suicide (NCPYS). https://www.preventyouthsuicide.org/programs.

> *"U OK?" Friends Ask! Suicide Prevention Program.* Peers engaging peers to prevent suicide. A fundraising and awareness model for youth to raise awareness and help prevent teen suicide.

Society for the Prevention of Teen Suicide (SPTS). Promotes a mission to reduce the number of youth suicides and attempted suicides by encouraging public awareness through the development and promotion of educational training programs. http://www.sptsusa.org.

> *Lifelines Intervention: Helping Students at Risk for Suicide.* Provides information on how to be prepared to address and respond to threats or signs of suicide and intervene.
> *Lifelines Prevention: Building Knowledge and Skills to Prevent Suicide.* Educates middle and high school faculty, parents, and students on the facts about suicide and their role in suicide prevention.
> *Lifelines Postvention: Responding to Suicide and Other Traumatic Death.* A program for the middle and high school community on how to successfully address and respond to suicide and other traumatic death that affects the school community.
> *Lifelines Trilogy: A Comprehensive Suicide Awareness and Responsiveness Program for Teens.*
> *Making Educators Partners in Youth Suicide Prevention.* In-person training of best practices, online training.
> *Training of Trainers.* Prepares participants to provide *Making Educators Partners in Youth Suicide Prevention (MEP)* training. Prerequisite: trainer candidates must complete the two-hour online module *Act on Facts: Making Educators Partners in Youth Suicide Prevention* prior to participating.

Suicide Awareness Voices of Education (SAVE). Engages the public by partnering with communities across the country to organize awareness events, start up new SAVE charters, and disseminate suicide prevention messaging. https://save.org.

> *LEADS for Youth.* A school-based suicide prevention curriculum designed for high schools and educators that links depression awareness and suicide prevention.
>
> *SMART—Students Mobilizing Awareness and Reducing Tragedies.* A suicide prevention program created for motivating student groups on high school and college campuses nationwide.

The Trevor Project is the leading national organization providing crisis intervention and suicide prevention services to lesbian, gay, bisexual, transgender, queer, and questioning (LGBTQ) young people under twenty-five. https://www.thetrevorproject.org.

> *LifeGuard Workshop.* A video training and curriculum to help educators, school counselors, nurses, and youth group leaders identify the challenges faced by LGBTQ people, to recognize the warning signs of suicide, and to respond to someone who may be in crisis.
>
> *Model School District Policy on Suicide Prevention.* A model schools and districts can use to implement suicide prevention policies. Fact sheet, full policy document, and webinar are available on The Trevor Project website.
>
> *Trevor Ally Trainings and Trevor CARE Trainings.* Training to help adults learn about LGBTQ youth, their risks and challenges, risk factors for suicide, protective factors, help, and support.

Yellow Ribbon Suicide Prevention Program. The Light for Life Foundation Int'l/Yellow Ribbon Suicide Prevention Program® is dedicated to preventing suicide and attempts by making suicide prevention accessible to everyone and removing barriers to help by empowering individuals and communities through leadership, awareness and education, and collaborating and partnering with support networks to reduce stigma and help save lives. https://yellowribbon.org/.

> *Ask 4 Help!*® Youth Suicide Prevention Training is a peer-based training that includes empowering the audience to learn to use this vital life skill. The presentations and trainings are built to increase help-seeking behaviors and links between peers and caring adults.
>
> *Youth Peer Leaders Training.* Communities have found that having youth trainers validates the importance of the topic among their peers, increases participation, and promotes cultural acceptance around help-seeking.

RELEVANT RESEARCH AND RESOURCES

2012 National Strategy for Suicide Prevention: Goals and Objectives for Action: A Report of the U.S. Surgeon General and of the National Action Alliance for Suicide Prevention. A report outlining a national strategy to guide suicide prevention actions. Includes up-to-date research on suicide prevention. https://www.hhs.gov/surgeongeneral/reports-and-publications/suicide-prevention/index.html.

Centers for Disease Control and Prevention. The Youth Risk Behavior Surveillance System monitors health-risk behaviors among youth, including a national school-based survey conducted by CDC and state, territorial, tribal, and local surveys conducted by state, territorial, and local education and health agencies and tribal governments. http://www.cdc.gov/healthyyouth/yrbs/index.htm.

Framework for Successful Messaging can be accessed at http://suicidepreventionmessaging.org/framework.

National Action Alliance for Suicide Prevention (Action Alliance) is working with more than 250 national partners from the public and private sectors to advance the National Strategy for Suicide Prevention (National Strategy). https://theactionalliance.org/.

National Council for Suicide Prevention (NCSP) includes a seven-member coalition. https://www.thencsp.org/.

> American Association of Suicidology (AAS)
> American Foundation for Suicide Prevention (AFSP)
> Samaritans USA
> SAVE—Suicide Voices of Education
> The Jason Foundation
> The JED Foundation
> The Trevor Project (LGBTQ youth)

Substance Abuse and Mental Health Services Administration (SAMHSA). Publications and Resources. https://www.samhsa.gov/suicide-prevention/publications-resources.

Suicide Prevention Resource Center (SPRC). www.sprc.org/.

> Assessing and Managing Suicide Risk (AMSR): https://www.sprc.org/training-events/amsr
> BeThe1To: http://www.bethe1to.com/bethe1to-steps-evidence/
> Online Suicide Prevention Courses:https://training.sprc.org/enrol/index.php?id=7
> State Prevention Plans:https://www.sprc.org/states
> Zero Suicide:https://www.sprc.org/zero-suicide

WORKING WITH THE MEDIA

American Foundation for Suicide Prevention and other leading partners. "Recommendations for Reporting on Suicide." http:// reportingonsuicide.org/.

Movement Advancement Project, Johnson Family Foundation, American Foundation for Suicide Prevention, Gay and Lesbian Alliance Against Defamation, and others. "Talking about Suicide and LGBT Populations." https://www.sprc.org/resources-programs/talking-about-suicide-and-lgbt-populations.

INTERVENTION: RECOMMENDED RESOURCES

A Friend Asks . . . How to Help a Friend. A phone app for students created by the Jason Foundation.

Kognito Simulation Program: At-Risk for PK—12 Educators. https://kognito.com/products/at-risk-for-high-school-educators.

Suicide in Schools: A Practitioner's Guide to Multi-level Prevention, Assessment, Intervention, and Postvention, by Terri A. Erbacher, Jonathan B. Singer, and Scott Poland.

Find research on successful interventions at Journalist's Resource. https://journalistsresource.org/home/suicide-prevention-research-on-successful-interventions/.

POSTVENTION: RECOMMENDED RESOURCES

After a Suicide: A Toolkit for Schools, 2nd ed. Suicide Prevention Resource Center. https://www.sprc.org/resources-programs/after-suicide-toolkit-schools.

Montana's CAST-S: The Montana Crisis Action School Toolkit on Suicide. https://dphhs.mt.gov/Portals/85/suicideprevention/CAST-S2017.pdf.

Suicide Prevention in Indian Country. SAMHSA Publications. https://store.samhsa.gov/product/Suicide-Prevention-in-Indian-Country/SMA16-4995.

Supporting Survivors of Suicide Loss: A Guide for Funeral Directors. Suicide Prevention Resource Center. https://www.sprc.org/resources-programs/help-hand-supporting-survivors-suicide-loss-guide-funeral-directors.

Children, Teens, and Suicide Loss. American Foundation for Suicide Prevention. https://afsp.org/find-support/ive-lost-someone/resources-loss-survivors/children-teens-suicide-loss/.

ENGAGING THE SCHOOL COMMUNITY: CONNECTEDNESS

#BeThe1To is the National Suicide Prevention Lifeline's message for National Suicide Prevention Month. Schools can customize the #BeThe1To phrase so it aligns with their efforts to build connectedness.

#BeThere is messaging promoted by the National Action Alliance for Suicide Prevention (Action Alliance) and its partners to highlight the role the public has in being there for others who might be struggling or in crisis. Use resources from the Action Alliance to help educate students about actions anyone, anywhere can take to make someone feel less alone.

Active Minds, Rachel's Challenge, and MindMatters are national organizations that work to help high school students and staff establish clubs that focus on connectedness along with mental health awareness and support.

School connectedness—the belief held by students that adults and peers in the school care about their learning as well as about them as individuals—is an important protective factor. Research has shown that young people who feel connected to their school are less likely to engage in many risk behaviors, including early sexual initiation; alcohol, tobacco, and other drug use; and violence and gang involvement. Students who feel connected to their school are also more likely to have better academic achievement, including higher grades and test scores, have better school attendance, and stay in school longer. Visit the CDC website to find Fact Sheets, a Strategy Guide, and a Staff Development program at https://www.cdc.gov/healthyyouth/protective/school_connect edness.htm.

Notes

1. A BRIEF HISTORY OF SUICIDE PREVENTION

1. Shneidman, Edwin, and Farberow, Norman, *The Los Angeles Suicide Prevention Center: A Demonstration of Public Health Feasibilities* (New York: American Public Health Association, 1965).

2. Resnik, H. L. P., and Hathorne, Berkley Charles, eds., *Suicide Prevention in the 70's* (Rockville, MD: National Institute of Mental Health, Center for Studies of Suicide Prevention, 1973).

3. U.S. Department of Health and Human Services, Alcohol, Drug Abuse, and Mental Health Administration, *Report of the Secretary's Task Force on Youth Suicide*, vol. 3: *Prevention and Interventions in Youth Suicide,* Pub. No. (ADM) 89-1623 (Washington, DC: Supt. Of Docs., U.S. Govt. Print. Off., 1989).

4. *Prevention of Suicide: Guidelines for the Formulation and Implementation of National Strategies* (New York: United Nations, 1996).

5. U.S. Public Health Service, *The Surgeon General's Call to Action to Prevent Suicide* (Washington, DC: DHHS, 1999).

6. U.S. Department of Health and Human Services, *National Strategy for Suicide Prevention: Goals and Objectives for Action* (Rockville, MD: Author, 2001).

7. Goldsmith, S., Pellmar, T., Kleinman, A., and Bunney, W., eds., *Reducing Suicide: A National Imperative* (Washington, DC: Institute of Medicine, The National Academies Press, 2002).

8. New Freedom Commission on Mental Health, *Achieving the Promise: Transforming Mental Health Care in America, Final Report*, Pub. No. SMA-03-3832 (Rockville, MD: DHHS, 2003).

9. Suicide Prevention Resource Center and Suicide Prevention Action Network USA, *Charting the Future of Suicide Prevention: A 2010 Progress Review of the National Strategy and Recommendations for the Decade Ahead,* ed. David Litts (Newton, MA: Education Development Center, 2010).

10. SPRC advances suicide prevention infrastructure and capacity building through:

- Consultation, training, and resources to enhance suicide prevention efforts in states, Native settings, colleges and universities, health systems and other settings, and organizations that serve populations at risk for suicide.

- Staffing, administrative, and logistical support to the Secretariat of the National Action Alliance for Suicide Prevention (Action Alliance), the public-private partnership dedicated to advancing the National Strategy for Suicide Prevention.
- Support for Zero Suicide, an initiative based on the foundational belief that suicide deaths for individuals under care within health and behavioral health systems are preventable. The initiative provides information, resources, and tools for safer suicide care (https://www.sprc.org/).

11. For a list of current grantees and examples of GLS grants, visit https://www.sprc.org/grantees.
12. Groups can use the National Suicide Prevention Lifeline social media campaign to create custom messages at http://www.bethe1to.com/join/.
13. The Action Alliance for Suicide Prevention is the nation's public-private partnership for suicide prevention. The Action Alliance works with more than 250 national partners to advance the National Strategy for Suicide Prevention. http://actionallianceforsuicideprevention.org/about-us.
14. *2012 National Strategy for Suicide Prevention: Goals and Objectives for Action: A Report of the U.S. Surgeon General and of the National Action Alliance for Suicide Prevention* (Washington, DC: U.S. Department of Health and Human Services, 2012), Sep. Appendix C, "Brief History of Suicide Prevention in the United States," https://www.ncbi.nlm.nih.gov/books/NBK109918/.
15. For current suicide statistics, visit AFSP at https://afsp.org/about-suicide/suicide-statistics/ or the CDC, www.cdc.gov.

2. THE CURRENT STATE OF SUICIDE PREVENTION IN SCHOOLS

1. Centers for Disease Control and Prevention, for current data visit https://www.cdc.gov/nchs/pressroom/sosmap/suicide-mortality/suicide.htm.
2. The Youth Risk Behavior Surveillance System (YRBSS) is often referred to as the Youth Risk Behavior Survey. Priority health-risk behaviors contribute to the leading causes of morbidity and mortality among youth and adults. Population-based data on these behaviors at the national, state, and local levels can help monitor the effectiveness of public health interventions designed to protect and promote the health of youth nationwide. Kann, Laura, et al., "Youth Risk Behavior Surveillance—United States, 2015," *Morbidity and Mortality Weekly Report* 65, no. 6 (June 10, 2016): 1–174, https://www.cdc.gov/mmwr/volumes/65/ss/ss6506a1.htm.
3. MOU refers to memorandum of understanding, or a written agreement with an agency or organization that will partner with a school to provide services.
4. Garrett Lee Smith Suicide Prevention grantees are funded by SAMHSA to support suicide prevention work in campus, state, and tribal communities. National Strategy for Suicide Prevention (NSSP) grantees are funded by SAMHSA to support states in implementing the 2012 National Strategy for Suicide Prevention on preventing suicide and suicide attempts among working-age adults twenty-five to sixty-four years old. Zero Suicide grantees are funded by the SAMHSA to support states, Indian tribes and tribal organizations, and health and behavioral health care organizations implementing comprehensive, multi-setting suicide prevention using the Zero Suicide model. To see examples of active grants, visit the Suicide Prevention Resource Center at https://www.sprc.org/grantees.
5. American Foundation for Suicide Prevention, "State Laws: Suicide Prevention in Schools (K–12) Issue Brief," August 30, 2018.
6. More Than Sad is an online video program that teaches teens, parents, and teachers about depression and mental health distress.
7. According to AFSP, every state has some form of suicide prevention training or awareness program available. However, the availability and accessibility of these programs vary. The

appeal of AFSP's Model Legislation on Suicide Prevention in Schools, and of the Jason Flatt Act, is that their language is worded to allow flexibility within states to choose the training programs that will best fit the educational environment(s) within their state.

AFSP offers several resources for schools that may be used to implement existing laws or to offset the cost of proposed legislation (fiscal note). This includes, but is not limited to, AFSP's More Than Sad educational program, AFSP's online Signs Matter program, and the jointly released *Model School District Policy on Suicide Prevention*. Details can be found online at http://afsp.org/our-work/education/. All resources are offered either as a free download online or through local AFSP chapters. [Eighty-five] AFSP chapters currently serve all fifty states across the United States. Find your local chapter online at http://afsp.org/our-work/chapters/.

8. The Suicide Prevention Resource Center is the only federally supported resource center devoted to advancing the implementation of the National Strategy for Suicide Prevention. SPRC is funded by the U.S. Department of Health and Human Services' Substance Abuse and Mental Health Services Administration (SAMHSA) and is located at the Education Development Center. https://www.sprc.org/.

9. The American Association of Suicidology's School Suicide Prevention Accreditation Program is for school personnel who serve as suicide prevention specialists. The program is designed for school psychologists, social workers, counselors, nurses, and all others dedicated to or responsible for reducing the incidence of suicide and suicidal behaviors among today's school-age youth. https://suicidology.org/training-accreditation/school-accreditation-program/.

10. The American Foundation for Suicide Prevention was founded on research. They develop evidence-based programs using the latest science on suicide prevention. Programs include training in mental health and suicide prevention for schools. https://afsp.org/our-work/education/.

11. Mental Health First Aid is an eight-hour course that teaches participants how to identify, understand, and respond to signs of mental illnesses and substance use disorders. The training teaches the skills needed to reach out and provide initial help and support to someone who may be developing a mental health or substance use problem or experiencing a crisis. https://www.mentalhealthfirstaid.org.

12. SafeTALK offers a half-day training program that teaches participants to recognize and engage persons who might be having thoughts of suicide and to connect them with community resources trained in suicide intervention. The "safe" in safeTALK stands for "suicide alertness for everyone"; "TALK" refers to practice actions used to help those with thoughts of suicide: Tell, Ask, Listen, and Keep Safe. https://www.sprc.org/resources-programs/suicide-alertness-everyone-safetalk.

13. ASIST's two-day workshop emphasizes the importance of teaching suicide first aid to help a person at risk stay safe and seek further help as needed. Participants learn to use a suicide intervention model to identify persons with thoughts of suicide, seek a shared understanding of reasons for dying and living, develop a safety plan based upon a review of risk, be prepared to do follow-up, and become involved in suicide-safer community networks. The learning process is based on adult learning principles and highly participatory. Graduated skills development occurs through mini-lectures, facilitated discussions, group simulations, and role plays.

14. The SOS Signs of Suicide Prevention Program is a youth suicide prevention program that has demonstrated an improvement in students' knowledge and adaptive attitudes about suicide risk and depression, as well as a reduction in actual suicide attempts. SOS is unique among school-based suicide prevention programs as it incorporates two prominent suicide prevention strategies into a single program: an educational curriculum that raises awareness about suicide and depression, and a brief screening for depression. The SOS programs use a simple acronym, ACT® (Acknowledge, Care, Tell), to teach students action steps to take if they encounter a situation that requires help from a trusted adult. SOS is offered for both middle and high school aged youth and can be implemented in one class period by existing faculty and staff. https://www.mentalhealthscreening.org/programs/youth.

15. More Than Sad for high school students teaches teens to recognize the signs of depression in themselves and others, challenges the stigma surrounding depression, and demystifies the treatment process. The program for parents teaches them how to recognize signs of depres-

sion and other mental health problems, initiate a conversation about mental health with their child, and get help. The teacher program shows educators how to recognize signs of mental health distress in students and refer them for help. The program complies with the requirements for teacher education suicide prevention training in many states. https://afsp.org/our-work/education/more-than-sad/.

16. Signs Matter: Early Detection will show educators how and when to express concern and refer students to counseling staff or administration. Signs Matter was developed based on a combination of science and best practice. The program presents scientifically based information on a variety of topics related to youth suicide, alongside best practice recommendations drawn from experts in the mental health and education fields. Science sheds light on key questions of risk and protective factors for youth suicide, as well as the most common behavioral presentations expressed by at-risk youth. Recommendations for school personnel roles, support, referrals, and interventions are drawn from best practices of educational and mental health experts. Signs Matter: Early Detection fulfills many states' requirements for educators to have two hours of instruction on suicide prevention and bullying. https://afsp.org/our-work/education/signs-matter-early-detection/. For a complete list of AFSP programs visit https://afsp.org/our-work/education/.

17. The Jason Foundation, Inc., series of online Staff Development Training Modules provide information on the awareness and prevention of youth suicide. These training modules are suitable for teachers, coaches, other school personnel, youth workers, first responders, foster parents, and any adult who works with or interacts with young people or wants to learn more about youth suicide. This series of programs introduces the scope and magnitude of the problem of youth suicide, the signs of concern, risk factors, how to recognize young people who may be struggling, how to approach the student and help an at-risk youth find resources for assistance.

The Jason Flatt Act is legislation that requires teachers and certain school personnel to complete two hours of youth suicide awareness and prevention training in order to maintain or renew their licensing credentials. The requirement for this training does not add additional hours of training, but rather falls within the number of hours already required to continue the professional teaching license. Twenty states have taken the initiative to be proactive in preventing youth suicide by passing the Jason Flatt Act: Tennessee, Louisiana, California, Mississippi, Illinois, Arkansas, Utah, South Carolina, West Virginia, Alaska, Ohio, North Dakota, Wyoming, Georgia, Montana, Texas, South Dakota, Alabama, and Kansas. https://jasonfoundation.com/get-involved/educator-youth-worker-coach/professional-development-series/.

18. The QPR Gatekeeper Training for Suicide Prevention is a brief in-person or online educational program designed to teach diverse audiences to recognize and refer someone at risk of suicide. Gatekeepers can include anyone who is strategically positioned to recognize and refer someone at risk of suicide (e.g., parents, friends, neighbors, teachers, coaches, caseworkers, police officers). The process follows three steps: (1) Question the individual's desire or intent regarding suicide, (2) Persuade the person to seek and accept help, and (3) Refer the person to appropriate resources. Trainees receive a QPR booklet and wallet card as a review and resource tool that includes local referral resources. https://qprinstitute.com/.

19. Kognito At-Risk for PK–12 Educators teaches elementary, middle, and high school teachers and other educators how to (1) identify students exhibiting signs of psychological distress, including depression, anxiety, substance abuse, and thoughts of suicide; (2) approach students to discuss their concern; and (3) make a referral to school support services. Through role-plays with animated and responsive avatars, participants engage in simulated conversations with three students of concern with the help of a virtual coach. In these virtual conversations, users learn effective conversation strategies for broaching the topic of psychological distress, motivating the student to seek help, and avoiding pitfalls, such as attempting to diagnose the problem or giving unwarranted advice. This online course is available from Kognito Interactive for a fee. https://kognito.com/products?markets=PK-12. See also their list of suicide prevention programs by state, https://kognito.com/articles/statewide-suicide-prevention-resources-is-your-state-on-the-list.

20. LEADS for Youth is a school-based suicide prevention curriculum designed for high schools and educators that links depression awareness and suicide prevention. LEADS for

Youth is an informative and interactive opportunity for students and teachers to increase knowledge and awareness of depression and suicide. LEADS is intended for students in grades nine through twelve and creates opportunities for conversations within the classroom around suicide and depression and the stigma surrounding suicide. Included in the curriculum are a teacher's guide, group and individual activities, suicide prevention resources, and a template for a school suicide crisis management plan. https://save.org/what-we-do/education/leads-for-youth-program/.

21. The Good Behavior Game is a universal classroom-based behavior management strategy for elementary school that teachers use along with a school's standard instructional curricula. GBG uses a game format with teams and rewards to socialize children to the role of student. It aims to reduce aggressive, disruptive classroom behavior, which is a shared risk factor for later problem behaviors, including adolescent and adult illicit drug abuse, alcohol abuse, cigarette smoking, antisocial personality disorder (ASPD), violent and criminal behavior, and suicidal thoughts and behaviors. https://www.goodbehaviorgame.org/.

22. Counseling on Access to Lethal Means (CALM) focuses on how access to lethal means can determine whether a person who is suicidal lives or dies. This course helps providers develop effective safety plans for people at risk of suicide. A Strategic Planning Approach to Suicide Prevention can help participants identify activities that will be effective in addressing the problem of suicide and assist with prioritizing efforts among the different options. Locating and Understanding Data for Suicide Prevention presents readily accessible sources of data that assist in understanding the suicide problem in educators' state or community and can help in determining which data are most useful for informing prevention activities. https://training.sprc.org/.

23. *To Live to See the Great Day That Dawns: Preventing Suicide by American Indian and Alaska Native Youth and Young Adults* can be downloaded at https://www.samhsa.gov/tribal-ttac/resources/suicide-prevention.

24. Through the Tribal Training and Technical Assistance (TTA) Center, SAMHSA provides culturally appropriate training and technical assistance to American Indian and Alaska Native (AI/AN) communities to address and prevent mental and substance use disorders and suicide and to promote mental health. The TTA guides tribal infrastructure development, capacity building, and program planning and implementation. https://www.samhsa.gov/tribal-ttac/tribal-training-technical-assistance.

25. Suicide prevention is a high priority for people working to promote wellness and reduce health disparities affecting American Indians and Alaska Natives (AI/AN). Drawing on strengths within Native traditions, community leaders and experts are developing models that are culturally based to promote mental health and prevent suicide for future generations. http://www.sprc.org/settings/aian.

26. Schools are a key setting for suicide prevention. Teachers, mental health providers, and all other school personnel who interact with students can play an important role in keeping them safe. https://www.sprc.org/settings/schools.

3. CHANGING THE MINDSET

1. The Susan B. Komen Breast Cancer Foundation, Inc. https://ww5.komen.org/Breastcancer/Understandingrisk.html.

2. National Alliance on Mental Illness (NAMI). https://www.nami.org/learn-more/mental-health-by-the-numbers.

3. The SOS Signs of Suicide Prevention Program is a universal, school-based depression awareness and suicide prevention program designed for middle school (ages 11–13) or high-school (ages 13–17) students. The goals are to (1) decrease suicide and suicide attempts by increasing student knowledge and adaptive attitudes about depression, (2) encourage personal help-seeking and/or help-seeking on behalf of a friend, (3) reduce the stigma of mental illness and acknowledge the importance of seeking help or treatment, (4) engage parents and school

staff as partners in prevention through "gatekeeper" education, and (5) encourage schools to develop community-based partnerships to support student mental health.

4. According to SPRC, schools are a key setting for suicide prevention. Teachers, mental health providers, and all other school personnel who interact with students can play an important role in keeping them safe. Maintaining a safe school environment is part of a school's overall mission. Students' mental health can affect how well they perform in school. Suicide can affect the entire school community. The best way to prevent suicide is to use a comprehensive approach that includes these key components: Promote emotional well-being and connectedness among all students. Identify students who may be at risk for suicide and assist them in getting help. Be prepared to respond when a suicide death occurs. To learn more visit https://www.sprc.org/settings/schools to see recommended resources.

5. The data shown represents average numbers in recent years. For current statistics visit https://www.cdc.gov/healthyyouth/data/yrbs/results.htm and look for the Trend Fact Sheet on suicide-related behaviors.

6. To bring Crisis Text Line to your community, school, or workplace, simply request a free Spread the Word Crisis Text Line Toolkit for schools at https://www.crisistextline.org/toolkit or email support@crisistextline.org. Crisis Trends collects and analyzes data from texters to learn more about how to combat mental illness. Schools and communities are encouraged to use the data to be proactive. Crisis Trends aims to empower journalists, researchers, school administrators, parents, and all citizens to understand the crises Americans face so we can work together to prevent future crises from happening. For more information visit https://crisistrends.org.

7. Fairfax County Public Schools in northern Virginia provide support to their students with a link that is easily found on the district's home page. Visit https://www.fcps.edu/student-wellness-tips.

8. https://everytownresearch.org/wp-content/uploads/2018/08/Suicide-FACT-SHEET-083019A.pdf.

9. According to the Suicide Prevention Resource Center, suicide prevention efforts can have greater power when they move beyond a single organization to reach a whole community. Find out what's going on in your state and consider ways to join with partners to have a greater impact. Find your state [listing] for information and resources, including contact information, suicide prevention plans, state and community organizations involved in suicide prevention, Garrett Lee Smith Suicide Prevention Act and National Strategy for Suicide Prevention (NSSP) grantees, and current legislation and news updates. https://www.sprc.org/states.

4. PREVENTION

1. The *Model School District Policy on Suicide Prevention* gives educators and school administrators a comprehensive way to implement suicide prevention policies in their local community. The policy, research-based and easily adaptable for middle and high schools, offers specific, actionable steps to support school personnel; sample language for student handbooks; suggestions for involving parents and guardians in suicide prevention; and guidance for addressing in-school suicide attempts. In addition to educators and school leaders, school-based mental health professionals such as counselors and psychologists are essential in putting a policy into practice to enhance the whole school environment. Download a free copy at https://afsp.org/our-work/education/model-school-policy-suicide-prevention/.

2. American School Counselor Association, *The Role of the School Counselor.* https://www.schoolcounselor.org/administrators/role-of-the-school-counselor.

3. American School Counselor Association, *ASCA National Model: A Framework for School Counseling Programs*, 4th ed., 2019, https://www.schoolcounselor.org/school-counselors-members/asca-national-model.

4. American Foundation for Suicide Prevention, *Model School District Policy on Suicide Prevention; Model Language, Commentary, and Resources*, revised 2018.

5. Centers for Disease Control and Prevention. (2010). Web-based Injury Statistics Query and Reporting System [Data file]. Retrieved from https://www.cdc.gov/injury/wisqars/index.html.

6. To find out about state laws on suicide prevention in K–12 schools, visit https://afsp.org/our-work/advocacy/public-policy-priorities/suicide-prevention-in-schools/. Select the link for the Suicide Prevention in Schools issue brief.

7. Find current statistics at https://afsp.org/about-suicide/suicide-statistics/.

8. The SOS Signs of Suicide Prevention Program (SOS) is a universal, school-based depression awareness and suicide prevention program designed for middle school (ages 11–13) or high school (ages 13–17) students. The goals are to (1) decrease suicide and suicide attempts by increasing student knowledge and adaptive attitudes about depression, (2) encourage personal help-seeking and/or help-seeking on behalf of a friend, (3) reduce the stigma of mental illness and acknowledge the importance of seeking help or treatment, (4) engage parents and school staff as partners in prevention through "gatekeeper" education, and (5) encourage schools to develop community-based partnerships to support student mental health.

9. Fairfax County Public Schools in northern Virginia provide support to their students with a link that is easily found on the district's home page. Visit https://www.fcps.edu/student-wellness-tips.

10. Reporting on Suicide.org lists many safe reporting recommendations. https://www.reportingonsuicide.org.

11. If your school has lost someone to suicide, *After a Suicide: A Toolkit for Schools* offers best practices and practical tools to help schools in the aftermath of a suicide. https://afsp.org/our-work/education/after-a-suicide-a-toolkit-for-schools/.

5. INTERVENTION

1. A suicide risk assessment should only be conducted by a mental health professional.

2. The National Association of School Psychologists (NASP) is a professional association that represents more than 25,000 school psychologists, graduate students, and related professionals throughout the United States and twenty-five other countries. The world's largest organization of school psychologists, NASP works to advance effective practices to improve students' learning, behavior, and mental health.

3. Communities in Schools provides school-based staff to partner with teachers to identify challenges students face in class or at home and coordinate with community partners to bring outside resources inside schools. From immediate needs like food or clothing to more complex ones like counseling or emotional support, they do whatever it takes to help students succeed. https://www.communitiesinschools.org.

4. Coalition for Community Schools: A community school is both a place and a set of partnerships between the school and other community resources. Its integrated focus on academics, health and social services, youth and community development, and community engagement leads to improved student learning, stronger families, and healthier communities. Community schools offer a curriculum that emphasizes real-world learning and community problem solving. Schools become centers of the community and are open to everyone—all day, every day, evenings, and weekends. http://www.communityschools.org.

5. Comprehensive Behavioral Health Model (CBHM) works to provide a setting where children, families, faculty, and community partners feel welcome and valued. Every child experiences a prosocial curriculum as part of the classroom and school experience. Teachers periodically review each of their students' behavioral health strengths and needs. Students in need of additional support are provided appropriate services in a timely fashion. Teams of teachers and administrators review student behavioral health data and progress on a regular basis. Community partners, families, and school personnel meet periodically and are in consistent communication about children that are receiving additional support. https://cbhmboston.com/what-is-cbhm/.

6. The NASP Model for Comprehensive and Integrated School Psychological Services, also known as the NASP Practice Model, represents NASP's official policy regarding the delivery of school psychological services. It delineates what services can reasonably be expected from school psychologists across ten domains of practice, and the general framework within which services should be provided. The recommended ratio for schools implementing this comprehensive model is 1 school psychologist for every 500 to 700 students.

6. POSTVENTION

1. The contents of this chapter are adapted from *After a Suicide: A Toolkit for Schools*, 2nd ed. (Waltham, MA: Education Development Center, Inc.), © 2018 Education Development Center, Inc., and American Foundation for Suicide Prevention. All rights reserved. Used with permission.

2. *After a Suicide: A Toolkit for Schools* is a publication by the American Foundation for Suicide Prevention (AFSP) in collaboration with the Suicide Prevention Resource Center (SPRC), Education Development Center (EDC), and endorsed by the National Association of Secondary School Principals (NASSP), the American School Counselor Association (ASCA), and the National Association of School Psychologists (NASP).

AFSP is the leading national not-for-profit organization exclusively dedicated to understanding and preventing suicide through research, education, and advocacy. AFSP's mission is to save lives and bring hope to those affected by suicide. https://afsp.org/.

SPRC is the nation's only federally supported resource center devoted to advancing the National Strategy for Suicide Prevention. It enhances the nation's mental health infrastructure by providing states, government agencies, private organizations, colleges and universities, and suicide survivor and mental health consumer groups with access to the science and experience that can support their efforts to develop programs, implement interventions, and promote policies to prevent suicide. https://www.sprc.org/.

3. To access the complete toolkit, visit http://www.sprc.org/resources-programs/after-suicide-toolkit-schools or https://afsp.org/our-work/education/after-a-suicide-a-toolkit-for-schools/.

4. Suicide is a public health issue. Media and online coverage of suicide should be informed by using best practices. Some suicide deaths may be newsworthy. However, the way media covers suicide can influence behavior negatively by contributing to contagion or positively by encouraging help-seeking behavior. Download recommendations for reporting on suicide at http://reportingonsuicide.org/.

5. The National Association of School Psychologists' School Safety and Crisis Response Committee provides phone, email, and onsite consultation. The National Institute for Trauma and Loss in Children (TLC) provides schools, agencies, and parents with names of TLC-certified trauma practitioners in their area who are available for consultation and referrals. TLC also has certified trauma trainers who can come to a school, organization, or community to provide training on suicide crisis response and postvention as well as other trauma-related topics. Call 877-306-5256 or email info@starr.org. The Dougy Center: National Center for Grieving Children & Families provides phone and onsite consultation and onsite training.

7. ENGAGING THE SCHOOL COMMUNITY IN SUICIDE PREVENTION

1. Teen Lifeline is a Phoenix, Arizona, nonprofit organization that provides peer counseling for teens in crisis. https://teenlifeline.org/get-involved/arizona-school-id-initiative/.

2. The Signs of Suicide Prevention Program (SOS) is a universal, school-based depression awareness and suicide prevention program designed for middle school (ages 11–13) or high school (ages 13–17) students. The goals are to (1) decrease suicide and suicide attempts by increasing student knowledge and adaptive attitudes about depression, (2) encourage personal help-seeking and/or help-seeking on behalf of a friend, (3) reduce the stigma of mental illness and acknowledge the importance of seeking help or treatment, (4) engage parents and school staff as partners in prevention through "gatekeeper" education, and (5) encourage schools to develop community-based partnerships to support student mental health.

3. "Counselor Crisis: Arizona Has the Highest Ratio of Students to School Counselors in the U.S.," *Arizona Republic*, August 14, 2018. https://www.azcentral.com/story/news/local/arizona-education/2018/08/14/arizona-has-highest-ratio-students-school-counselors-united-states/889833002/.

4. "School Connectedness," Adolescent and School Health, July 2009, https://www.cdc.gov/healthyyouth/protective/school_connectedness.htm.

5. The *Model School District Policy on Suicide Prevention* gives educators and school administrators a comprehensive way to implement suicide prevention policies in their local community. https://afsp.org/our-work/education/model-school-policy-suicide-prevention/.

6. Substance Abuse and Mental Health Services Administration, *Preventing Suicide: A Toolkit for High Schools*, HHS Publication No. SMA-12-4669 (Rockville, MD: Center for Mental Health Services, Substance Abuse and Mental Health Services Administration, 2012).

7. *Youth Suicide Prevention, Intervention, and Postvention Guidelines: A Resource for School Personnel* (https://www.sprc.org/states/maine) and the *Youth Suicide Prevention Referral and Tracking Toolkit* (http://www.sprc.org/resources-programs/youth-suicide-prevention-referral-and-tracking-toolkit) are both available from the SPRC website.

8. *Montana's CAST-S Crisis Action School Toolkit on Suicide*, 2017, https://saom.memberclicks.net/assets/SAM_unpublished_links/CAST-S%202017%20FINAL_revised.pdf.

8. SUCCESS STORIES

1. Sasha Jones, "Schools Are Required to Teach Mental Health Lessons This Fall in Two States," *Education Week*, September 25, 2018, http://blogs.edweek.org/edweek/curriculum/2018/08/schools_required_to_teach_mental_health_ny_va.html?cmp=eml-enl-cm-news2&M=58582316&U=1986086.

2. The National Violent Death Reporting System (NVDRS) provides states and communities with a clearer understanding of violent deaths to guide local decisions about efforts to prevent violence and track progress over time. NVDRS is the only state-based surveillance (reporting) system that pools data on violent deaths from multiple sources into a usable, anonymous database. These sources include state and local medical examiner, coroner, law enforcement, toxicology, and vital statistics records. NVDRS covers all types of violent deaths—including homicides and suicides—in all settings and for all age groups. NVDRS may include data on mental health problems; recent problems with a job, finances, or relationships; physical health problems; and information about circumstances of death. Such data is far more comprehensive than what is available elsewhere.

3. Suicide Prevention Lifeline, "Stories of Hope and Recovery," https://suicidepreventionlifeline.org/stories/.

4. Purtill, Corinne, "Suicide Hotlines Really Do Save Lives. I Know Because One Saved Mine," September 9, 2018, https://qz.com/1381952/suicide-hotlines-really-do-save-lives-i-know-because-one-saved-mine/.

5. Gould, Madelyn S., et al., "Follow-Up with Callers to the National Suicide Prevention Lifeline: Evaluation of Callers' Perceptions of Care," *Suicide and Life-Threatening Behavior* 48, no. 1 (2017), https://onlinelibrary.wiley.com/doi/abs/10.1111/sltb.12339.

6. King, Cheryl A., et al., "Association of the Youth-Nominated Support Team Intervention for Suicidal Adolescents With 11- to 14-Year Mortality Outcomes," *JAMA Psychiatry* 76, no. 5 (February 2019): 492–98, https://www.ncbi.nlm.nih.gov/pubmed/30725077.

7. Asarnow, Joan R., et al., "Cognitive-Behavioral Family Treatment for Suicide Attempt Prevention: A Randomized Controlled Trial," *Journal of the American Academy of Child & Adolescent Psychiatry* 56, no. 6 (June 2017): 506–14, https://www.ncbi.nlm.nih.gov/pubmed/28545756.

8. McCauley, Elizabeth, et al., "Efficacy of Dialectical Behavior Therapy for Adolescents at High Risk for Suicide," *JAMA Psychiatry*, 75, no. 8 (August 2018): 777–85, https://www.ncbi.nlm.nih.gov/pubmed/29926087.

9. Schilling, Elizabeth A., Aseltine, Robert H., and James, Amy, "The SOS Suicide Prevention Program: Further Evidence of Efficacy and Effectiveness," *Prevention Science* 17, no. 2 (February 2016): 157–66, https://www.ncbi.nlm.nih.gov/pubmed/26314868.

10. Van der Zande, Irene, "Suicide Prevention Success Story: The Opposite of Cyberbullying," *Kidpower*, May 2, 2013, https://www.kidpower.org/library/article/suicide-prevention-success-story/.

11. Utah Department of Health, Violence and Injury Prevention Program, "Data Help Describe Suicide Problem in Utah," https://vetoviolence.cdc.gov/apps/successstories/show-doc.aspx?s=3073&dt=0.

12. See *NVDRS: Stories from the Frontlines of Violent Death Surveillance* (Atlanta, GA: Safe States Alliance, 2013), https://cdn.ymaws.com/www.safestates.org/resource/resmgr/NVDRS/NVDRS_Stories_-_2015.pdf.

13. American Foundation for Suicide Prevention, "State Statutes—Suicide Prevention in Schools," July 17, 2017.

14. American Foundation for Suicide Prevention, https://afsp.org/our-work/advocacy/.

15. Suicide is a public health issue. Media and online coverage of suicide should be informed by using best practices. The way media covers suicide can influence behavior negatively by contributing to contagion, or positively by encouraging help-seeking. See Reporting on Suicide.org, http://reportingonsuicide.org/.

9. WHAT THE FUTURE WILL BE

1. See the section on Suicide Prevention Organizations and Programs in chapter 10, "Resources."

2. The *Model School District Policy on Suicide Prevention* gives educators and school administrators a comprehensive way to implement suicide prevention policies in their local community. In collaboration with the American School Counselor Association, the National Association of School Psychologists, and The Trevor Project, the program is research-based, and easily adaptable for middle and high schools. There are specific, actionable steps to support school personnel; sample language for student handbooks; suggestions for involving parents and guardians in suicide prevention; and guidance for addressing in-school suicide attempts. In addition to educators and school leaders, school-based mental health professionals such as counselors and psychologists are essential in putting a policy into practice to enhance the whole school environment. More than half of all states in the United States currently require that educators receive training to prevent suicide. With recommendations rooted in best practices, the *Model School District Policy on Suicide Prevention* can complement state law requirements and help schools achieve an inclusive, comprehensive suicide prevention plan. https://afsp.org/our-work/education/model-school-policy-suicide-prevention/.

3. Marshall, Doreen S., et al., *After a Suicide: A Toolkit for Schools*, 2nd ed (Waltham, MA: Education Development Center, Inc.), American Foundation for Suicide Prevention, Suicide Prevention Resource Center, Education Development Center, 2018. If your school has lost someone to suicide, *After a Suicide* offers best practices and practical tools to help schools in the aftermath of a suicide. This toolkit can help schools respond in the aftermath of a suicide death. The second edition provides information for school administrators and other school staff who wish to implement a coordinated response to the suicide. The toolkit provides information on how best to communicate and support the school community and manage the crisis response. Also found in the toolkit is information on helping students cope, communicating with

parents, working with the community, and engaging external resources for support. While designed primarily for school personnel, the toolkit also contains useful guidance for parents and communities. https://afsp.org/our-work/education/after-a-suicide-a-toolkit-for-schools/.

4. The PAX Good Behavior Game® is an evidence-based practice consisting of instructional and behavioral health strategies used daily by teachers and students in the classroom. This preventive approach not only improves classroom behavior and academics, but also benefits children by improving self-regulation and co-regulation with peers. More information is available at https://www.goodbehaviorgame.org/.

5. Dialectical behavior therapy (DBT) skills have been demonstrated to be effective in helping adolescents manage difficult emotional situations, cope with stress, and make better decisions. http://www.dbtinschools.com/.

6. Signs Matter presents scientifically based information on a variety of topics related to youth suicide, alongside best practice recommendations drawn from experts in the mental health and education fields. The program addresses risk and protective factors for youth suicide, as well as the most common behavioral presentations expressed by at-risk youth. Recommendations for school personnel roles, support, referrals, and interventions are drawn from best practices of educational and mental health experts. More information is available at https://afsp.org/our-work/education/signs-matter-early-detection/.

7. Sources of Strength is a youth suicide prevention project designed to use peer social networks to change unhealthy norms and culture. This model strengthens multiple sources of support (protective factors) around young individuals by increasing help-seeking behaviors and promoting connections between peers and caring adults. More information is available at https://sourcesofstrength.org/.

8. PBIS is funded by the U.S. Department of Education's Office of Special Education Programs (OSEP) and the Office of Elementary and Secondary Education (OESE). The Technical Assistance Center on PBIS supports schools, districts, and states to build systems capacity for implementing a multi-tiered approach to social, emotional, and behavior support. The broad purpose of PBIS is to improve the effectiveness, efficiency, and equity of schools and other agencies. PBIS improves social, emotional, and academic outcomes for all students, including students with disabilities and students from underrepresented groups. https://www.pbis.org/.

9. Responsive Classroom is an evidence-based approach to teaching that focuses on engaging academics, positive community, effective management, and developmental awareness. Workshops, books, and resources help elementary and middle school educators create safe and joyful learning communities where students develop strong social and academic skills and every student can thrive. Independent research has found that the Responsive Classroom approach is associated with higher academic achievement in math and reading, improved school climate, and higher-quality instruction. It has been described by the Collaborative for Academic, Social, and Emotional Learning (CASEL) as one of the most "well-designed evidence-based social and emotional learning (SEL) programs."

10. The StigmaFree campaign is NAMI's effort to end stigma and create hope for those affected by mental illness. https://nami.org/stigmafree.

About the Author

Theodora Schiro received her BS in elementary education from Virginia Commonwealth University and her MEd in school administration from the University of Massachusetts. She served as a public school teacher and administrator for over thirty-six years.

After leaving the public education world, Theodora started a freelance writing business. Skilled in writing content that helps businesses, public service organizations, and nonprofits, she has been published on company websites and in the ASCD journal, *Educational Leadership*.

To help her recover from the loss of her son in the spring of 2011, Theodora joined the American Foundation for Suicide Prevention (AFSP). Determined to address the stigma of suicide and increase public awareness of depression and other mental illnesses, she is actively working to educate school personnel in suicide prevention.

www.ingramcontent.com/pod-product-compliance
Lightning Source LLC
Chambersburg PA
CBHW021537260326
41914CB00001B/53